HOW TO GET
FILTHY, STINKING
RICH
AND STILL HAVE TIME FOR
GREAT SEX

HOW TO GET FILTHY, STINKING RICH AND STILL HAVE TIME FOR GREAT SEX

HERB KAY

Bard Press

AUSTIN

HOW TO GET FILTHY, STINKING RICH AND STILL HAVE TIME FOR GREAT SEX
An Entrepreneur's Guide to Wealth and Happiness

Copyright © 2000 by Herb Kay. All rights reserved.
Printed in the United States of America.
Permission to reproduce or transmit in any form or by any means, electronic or mechanical, including photocopying and recording, or by an information storage and retrieval system, must be obtained by writing to the publisher at the address below:

Bard Press
1515 S. Capital of Texas Highway, Suite 107
Austin, TX 78746
512-329-8373 voice, 512-329-6051 fax
www.bardpress.com

Ordering Information
To order additional copies, contact your local bookstore or call 800-945-3132. Quantity discounts are available.
ISBN 1-885167-36-9 hardcover

Library of Congress Cataloging-in-Publication Data
Kay, Herb, 1957-
  How to get filthy, stinking rich and still have time for great sex :
an entrepreneur's guide to wealth and happiness / Herb Kay.
    p. cm.
  ISBN 1-885167-36-9 (hardcover)
  1. New business enterprises--Management. 2. Success in business.

  HD62.5 .k39 2000
  658.1'141--dc21   00-022790

The author may be contacted at the following address:
Herb Kay
5151 E. Broadway Blvd., Ste. 790
Tucson, AZ 85711
520-750-1111 voice, 520-750-1177 fax
HKRichMaster@aol.com

Credits
Developmental editor: **Amy Reznik**
Editor: **Jeff Morris**
Proofreaders: **Letitia Blalock, Deborah Costenbader**
Index: **Linda Webster**
Cover design: **Hespenheide Design**
Text design/production: **Jeff Morris**
Digital imagery © copyright 1999 PhotoDisc, Inc.

First printing: March 2000

Taking the risk to be a successful entrepreneur is possible only if the foundation upon which you build the rest of your life is sound. Opposition to your plans by those closest to you, or family strife of any kind, can only serve to weaken and distract you from your chosen course. I have had to deal with nothing like that, because my foundation and the love of my life, my wife Terri, has never been anything but a source of strength and warmth.

Terri sets me straight when my path grows indistinct. She counsels me unerringly about whom I can trust. She is the world's best judge of character. She has made our home an oasis of peace and tranquility. Most of all, she is the best wife and life partner I can imagine. To know her is to love her, and I am not alone in this feeling; she still has friends from grade school. A friend of Terri's is a friend for life!

I dedicate this book to you, my darling.

CONTENTS

PART II. CHOOSE YOUR FUTURE (Planning Your Arrival)

PART III. MAKE IT WORK (Growing Your Dough)

PART IV. MAKE TIME FOR GREAT SEX (...and Other Important Things in Life)

ABOUT THE AUTHOR

(THINGS YOU SHOULD KNOW ABOUT HERB KAY)

Fly to sunny Tucson, cross the border into Mexico, drive to the town of Puerto Peñasco nestled like a jewel on the Sea of Cortez, find the exclusive gated community of Las Conchas, and there you're likely to find Herb Kay, his wife

Terri, and their four children at their beach home enjoying the benefits of being Filthy, Stinking Rich while still having time for Great Sex. Or he might save you the trip by flying you there personally in his private plane. And if you don't find him there, he might just as easily be at his youngest son's chess tournament, his little girl's violin recital, his oldest son's golf tournament, or out for a fun evening with his oldest daughter. Herb has spent his adult life accumulating wealth, but he's no workaholic, and he thinks that no one ever should be. He has learned the hard way what's really important and has dedicated his professional life to helping others achieve both wealth and happiness.

Born in Miami Beach and raised in Pittsburgh, Herb rebelled at seventeen, joined the Navy, became a Russian linguist, learned to fly, started a retail business, failed, started over, ruined a marriage, built a successful investment business, and hosted a TV talk show. He now appears nationally as a TV financial expert, starts new ventures, makes lots of money as an entrepreneur, manages millions of dollars for people all over the country, is married to the love of his life, and lives happily ever after with his family. And he does all of this using his experience and common sense. He dropped out of college his freshman year and never looked back.

ACKNOWLEDGMENTS

(PEOPLE WHO HELPED HERB KAY)

I would like to express my love and deep thanks to Amy Reznik, who was my "ghost" for this book. Though every word of the book is my own, it is Amy who did lots of hard work in committing my thoughts to paper. I have known Amy since she was fourteen years old and in braces, and after she graduated with a degree in creative writing from the University of Arizona, I knew that she was the one to help me with this book. There are a lot of professional writers out there who would have been acceptable for the project, but only Amy could think and write in my voice with integrity. I know that her future is so bright that she'll have to wear shades!

If a man has one really good friend in a lifetime, he is lucky, and in this regard I have been super-blessed, as I have a few. One of them is Mark Batterman, my personal manager and good friend, the man who did no less than set me on the path that led to my media career and this book. More than just professionally, he's been the guiding light of my life. He's the best!

I would also like to acknowledge all of those early investors in my business ventures, some going back nearly two decades: namely, Dean Goss, General George and Mrs. Kitty Williams, Captain Thomas and Mrs. Eileen Copeman, Dr. Wesley and Mrs. Genevieve Murbach, Ms. Marilyn Bedell, Paul and Helen Hermes, and Otto Olsson, who not only has assisted me as an investor but has served as my mentor. He has been the father figure missing in my life, as well as a loyal confidant.

And, of course, along the way I've had lots of super advisors who have also been my friends, like CPAs Matt Osburn and Dominick Angiulo, my attorney Carmine Cornelio, and my banker, Jeff Walters. I couldn't have done it without them.

No list of acknowledgments would be complete without my publisher, Ray Bard, and my agent, Carol Susan Roth. Thanks for looking closely enough to see that what I had was a lot more than a cute title. I also want to thank my editor, Jeff Morris. I had real fear about letting someone mess with my "art." I shouldn't have worried. Jeff just made it better.

Finally, there are my children: Lindsay, Jonathan, Julian, and Chloe. No matter how happy a person is on a regular basis, there are inevitably days when you feel kind of low. There is no sugar-coating what it feels like to fail at something, big or small. When that happens, the sure cure is unconditional love, and my children have that for me, and I for them, in unlimited supply. They are the reason I get up every morning and face the world with a smile.

PART I

THE ROAD TO RICHES

(Big Picture Stuff)

1
LITTLE MONEY VS. BIG MONEY

(DEFINING "FILTHY, STINKING RICH")

There are three ways to get rich: slow, fast, and smart. This book is about getting rich smart. I won't waste much time on slow or quick. I'll leave those subjects for other people's books (*How to Get Rich by Making Yourself Miserable* and *How to Get Rich by Falling for Every Sucker Bet That Comes Your Way*). I'm going to show you a much better way.

Oh, sure, you can make money investing in stocks or real estate. I have. But you've got to have money to start with, and you'll need lots of time. Getting rich smart, on the other hand, doesn't take a lot of money, and it won't take you the rest of your life. All it takes is know-how, and I can help you with that.

First, a definition. What do I mean by "filthy, stinking rich"? Exactly how much money is that? A million dollars? Five million? Ten million? It depends. When talking about wealth, we need to distinguish between the two types of "rich": little money and big money.

LIVING SMALL

Little money is the kind of money that people can save toward over a long time. To achieve little money is to gradually accumulate an estate worth two or three million dollars. If that's your goal, and if you're an average person with an average income who works for someone else, little money is a realistic goal. It just means that you have to save and invest slowly and methodically for forty years. Do you want to wait forty years to be rich?

When you retire with a couple of million bucks, you can have a safe annual income of $100,000 or so, based on the interest paid on treasury bills. With that much money you could have a nice, comfortable lifestyle and still have enough left over to play a round of golf each week and go visit the grandkids on their birthdays. That's a decent income, but it's not a filthy-stinking-rich income.

CAN'T LOSE FOR WINNING

Big money is a whole other thing. Big money is filthy, stinking rich. But filthy, stinking rich is not a number — it's a lifestyle! The filthy, stinking rich way of life consists of making a lot of money and not having to wait until you're sixty-five to enjoy it. Without putting a dollar amount on it, to be filthy, stinking rich is to have so much money that money doesn't matter anymore — to have so much money that you don't need a budget. That's not possible with the two or three million dollars you save as the millionaire next door.

Filthy, stinking rich is not a number — it's a lifestyle!

When you're filthy, stinking rich, everything you buy just keeps making you more money. You buy risky stocks, they make you money. You buy a vacation home in the Bahamas, it makes you money. You buy a jet, it makes you money. There doesn't seem to be any way to get rid of it. Sure, if you decide to buy a country or a planet or something, you might first want to check the balance in your bank account, but for the most 19 part you're pretty safe buying anything you want without worrying about it. Of course, there's no accounting for sheer stupidity, but I have faith in you.

A NEW WAY OF LIVING

More than anything else, filthy, stinking rich is a mindset. For example, I wanted to be rich, and I wanted it to happen before I was using a walker and gumming my food, but investing and saving methodically would have taken too long. The only way I could make money fast enough was to have an ambitious, filthy-stinking-rich attitude and go into business for myself.

Filthy, stinking rich. You want an exact number, don't you? A figure to keep in the back of your head. All right, let's say $10 million in total *liquid* assets. The interest alone would make you $500,000 or so a year, more than most people can conceivably spend. Try spending $40,000 a month, every month, for the rest of your life. It may be fun at first, but it gets tiring fast. Ten million dollars. That, my friend, is filthy, stinking rich.

You're thinking that's a lot of money. Yes. An unattainable amount? No. You see, the funny thing about getting filthy, stinking rich is that the only difficult threshold to cross is getting rich. Once you've adopted the habit of being self-sufficient and just a little bit aggressive, bridging the gap between rich and filthy, stinking rich does not require that big a leap.

Once you've adopted the habit of being self-sufficient and just a little bit aggressive, bridging the gap between rich and filthy, stinking rich does not require that big a leap.

After the first two or three million, it's just a hop, skip, and a jump to ten million.

It's important to understand that it doesn't take great genius to turn a mountain of money into a big mountain of money. All it takes is the know-how to make the first mountain. After that, it's easy. The big mountain almost builds itself.

20

MONEY IS FUN

We live in a society where if you make money you're supposed to act like you don't. You're supposed to say things like "Oh, I don't care about the money" and "Money doesn't mean anything to me." Of course money means something!

Money isn't everything, but let's be honest — it is something. Something big. Even people who don't care about the money care about the money. And there's nothing wrong with that. There is nothing wrong — in the Bible, in religion, in life — with being rich. It's fun.

You know the old saying "Money can't buy happiness"? Well, maybe not. But it can buy time, and time translates into freedom — the freedom to pursue happiness and personal growth, the freedom to help others. Don't buy into that silly mentality of rich people not being happy. Let me assure you, you can be pretty damn happy with a few million bucks.

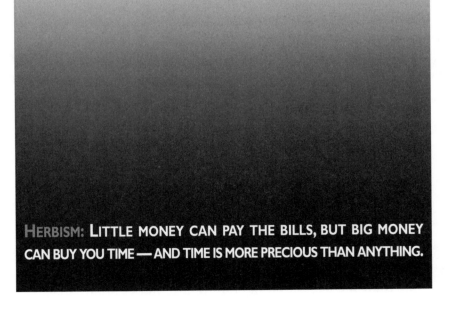

HERBISM: LITTLE MONEY CAN PAY THE BILLS, BUT BIG MONEY CAN BUY YOU TIME — AND TIME IS MORE PRECIOUS THAN ANYTHING.

2
GETTING RICH QUICK

(IF IT'S SO EASY, WHY AIN'T EVERYBODY RICH?)

Most of us have heard or seen Nick GetRichQuick. He works forty hours a week at the same cubicle job he's had for eight years, where he spends a large part of his day surfing the Internet for the hot investing story of the moment.

He secretly sneers at his supervisors in their offices, bitter at their success. Every week he spends $20 on lottery tickets, always picking the same numbers, convinced that someday his combination will be the winning one. Nick's credit card bills are high, due mostly to the plethora of gadgets and books he orders from late-night infomercials and weekend seminars promising him the secrets to instant wealth. Nick is a paranoid, money-hungry, miserable jerk.

22 Sound familiar? I'm sure you know at least one or two people like Nick, whose only goal in life is to make money. They see life as a racetrack with money at the finish line, and they're unable to focus on anything else. They hop from scheme to scheme, desperately searching for the well-kept secret that will magically make them wealthy overnight. I've got tough news for the Nicks of the world: There ain't no such thing.

FREE MONEY — ACT FAST!

Perhaps a profile of a typical get-rich-quick scheme will help to illustrate my point. Dozens of these self-proclaimed gurus and systems have come and gone over the years, and they're all the same. They always imply that it's possible to get something for nothing, and that they can show you how. **Red Flag #1:** There is no such thing as something for nothing, no matter how earnest their promises.

In defense of people who fall for these get-rich-quick programs, some of them are difficult to spot as scams. A seemingly trustworthy person, with degrees of various kinds from one university or another, insists he was just like you until this wonderful system changed his life. The sales pitch can be pretty convincing. But whenever he suggests something for nothing, run for the hills.

> **In defense of people who fall for these get-rich-quick programs, some of them are difficult to spot as scams.**

He sweetens the deal by gushing about how unbelievably easy it is: "Anyone can do it! This fantastic program requires no special skills or training, and not a penny in cash! It can all be conveniently charged to your Visa or MasterCard!" (Forget about that silly little 18 percent interest rate.) "This investment will pay you back a thousandfold!"

He reels you in with the promise that he's going to reveal the industry's hidden secrets. You know — the ones the experts know but aren't sharing. This approach appeals to the green-eyed monster in all of us. There's nothing like the idea of others

getting theirs, while you're getting nothing, to get that green 23
blood boiling! **Red Flag #2:** If this "secret system" were so easy
to use and so obvious, it wouldn't be a secret. Everyone and his
dog would be rich, including the fleas.

And, of course, this is all a risk-free venture. He guarantees
it as vehemently as possible without actually guaranteeing it.
On the off chance that he even mentions risk, it's only in
passing. "Well, there's a teeny, tiny, itsy, bitsy chance that it
won't work, *but look back over here at how much money you
can make if it does work!*" It's always a game of "keep your eye
on the get-rich-quick ball." **Red Flag #3:** There's no such thing
as risk-free reward.

THE LESSONS OF HISTORY

I can shoot down every get-rich-quick scheme with two
statements. The first is that there is no hidden system for
playing the stock market or investing anywhere else. How
do I know? It's really very simple. Every type of investing —
stocks, bonds, futures, real estate — depends on middlemen.
The only way these people make
serious money is on commissions.
All get-rich-quick schemes are
frenetic; there's a lot of buying
and selling going on. With all
that movement, brokers stand
to make a fortune! It doesn't
matter whether you're making
a bundle or losing it — any move
you make means a commission

> **Get-rich-quick schemes are
> founded in desperation. People
> who subscribe to them are
> frantic to make money, and to
> make it right now!**

for your broker. Believe me, faced with that opportunity, thousands of middlemen should be shouting the "secret system"
from the rooftops.

Second, there is no better judge than history. Look at the
track records of the wealthiest people in the world, past and
present — people like John D. Rockefeller, J. P. Morgan, Sam
Walton, and Bill Gates. None of them made their money in a
quick scheme. They earned it through business. There's nothing

24   hidden or secret about it. And if you ever investigate a get-rich-quick guru's claim that whatever system he's selling worked for him, you'll find it's not true. That's what always brings down these charlatans — they're found never to have done any such thing.

Get-rich-quick schemes are founded in desperation. People who subscribe to them are frantic to make money, and to make it right now! They are afraid and paranoid that if they don't get their hands on it immediately, the opportunity may pass them by. They have to get theirs before someone else gets to it first.

That's not how it works, folks. There's no race to get to "your share" of the money. More wealth is created every day. If you don't make it today, you can make it tomorrow. The right way. The way that really works: through business. Making money is something that takes time. It doesn't happen overnight.

HERBISM: NO ONE GETS SOMETHING FOR NOTHING. IT'S AGAINST THE LAWS OF NATURE.

3

GETTING RICH SLOW

(THE WHEELS OF FORTUNE GRIND EXCEEDINGLY FINE)

Everybody knows Joe GetRichSlow. Much like Nick GetRichQuick, Joe works at the same cubicle job he's had for eight years, but unlike his colleague, he puts in overtime every week.

Each day on his lunch break, he calls his financial advisor to check on the progress of his portfolio, detailing each small change in a file that he keeps on his computer. On coffee breaks, he eavesdrops on his supervisors' discussions about the stock market. Every month he puts exactly $200 into a mutual fund, invests $200 in stocks, and puts $100 into his savings account. Although he makes a good living, Joe lives in a small apartment, drives the same car he had in college, and rarely takes vacations. Joe is uptight, stressed out, and too wound up to relax.

LIVING WITH SCARCITY

Getting rich slow is also known as getting rich safe. You can find shelves of books outlining different versions of this, but they all call for basically the same behaviors: Live beneath your means. Buy less than you can afford. Control your debt. Save as much money as you can. Invest in good things and hold onto them for a long time. Allow the miracle of compound interest to work for you, and when you finally retire at sixty-five, you'll have 1.8742 million dollars.

> **The entire concept of carefully investing and watching every penny stems from the Depression, when everything was scarce.**

If the get-rich-quick theory is the desperation model of achieving wealth, getting rich slow is the scarcity model. It's based on the fear that there won't be enough to go around. The entire concept of carefully investing and watching every penny stems from the Depression, when everything was scarce. People were afraid their resources would run out at any moment, so they stockpiled them.

Getting rich slow adheres to the same concept, and it's a very popular approach these days. Most people who are working toward wealth subscribe to this model. It's safe, it's practical, and it's worry-free. But that doesn't necessarily make it the best approach.

THE WAY OF THE TORTOISE

Although it's sound in theory, getting rich slow has three big strikes against it. First, it's slow! I don't want to wait twenty, thirty, forty years to enjoy the fruits of my hard work. Working for someone else, investing meticulously, counting every penny — that doesn't sound like a fun way to spend the major part of my life. Does it sound like fun to you?

Second, not everyone lives far beyond sixty-five. According to the National Center for Health Statistics, the life expectancy for a man of my ethnicity and age is about sixty-seven years. So let 27 me get this straight: I work hard all my life and save my pennies for a comfortable retirement at sixty-five, only to die two years later? When do I get to relax with my loved ones and enjoy the comfort that we've worked so hard to attain? I could check out tomorrow. So regardless of how faithfully I eat my broccoli, take my vitamins, exercise, and floss, I could still die unexpectedly in an accident (the most common cause of death for people under sixty-five) and never have the opportunity to enjoy the money I've saved so diligently.

The third and final thing wrong with getting rich slow is the habits you establish in the process. Getting rich slow can work. Saving, investing, and curbing your spending habits is a legitimate means to a safe and predictable end. But take it from a man who spends a large part of his day managing the money of retirees who got rich slow: it is psychologically difficult, if not impossible, for many of them to enjoy the wealth they've accumulated.

OLD HABITS OUTLIVE YOU

Human beings are creatures of habit. After a lifetime of being one way, it's hard to cross the finish line of retirement and magically change to another way of living. As often as not, forty years of counting and saving every penny will wind you up so tight you'll squeak and suffer permanent constipation. I've had many retirees come to me proud of the money they've saved but unable to do anything with it.

I have a client in Texas who has done just that. She and her late husband spent their whole life together working hard and saving to retire with a couple of million bucks — which now, thanks to yours truly, has grown to a lot more. Each month, $50,000 is automatically deposited into her checking account, and each month — without fail — she calls me to ask me what she should do with it. My answer has become so predictable that she interrupts me before I even open my mouth: "And, Herb, don't tell me to take a cruise!" It's become a joke between us. She's eighty-five and has a pacemaker, but otherwise she's

28 in perfect health. She could easily enjoy a cruise, or a vacation, or a shopping spree, but she won't do it. Instead, she spends her days just as she did for the past fifty years: she stays at home cutting coupons and knitting. It makes me sad.

The bottom line: getting rich slow works. If you can adhere to the strict rules and play the game just the way you're supposed to, you can save your way to a million bucks. But what good is a million bucks if you've had to live a miserable life to get there? The time to have fun is now, not forty years from now. Who wants to wait forty years to be rich?

HERBISM: OUR FOREFATHERS CAME TO AMERICA TO PARTY, NOT TO LIVE LIKE MONKS.

4
GETTING RICH SMART

(BUYING TIME TO ENJOY LIFE)

Now meet my pal Art GetRichSmart. Dissatisfied with the lack of personal freedom and limiting paycheck of his cubicle job, Art left a year ago to start his own business. An avid biker, he decided to make his passion his livelihood. After drawing up a solid business plan and gaining the support of investors, he opened up his own bike shop.

Although Art was a bit nervous at first, business has grown steadily and he has never been happier. He's in control of his career and looks forward to the challenges that each new day of running his own business brings. At the moment he has less personal income than he had at his cubicle job, but if business

30   continues to grow for the next year, he'll double his income and be able to open another shop across town.

The thought of building and expanding his own business keeps Art happy and satisfied with his career. And since he's his own boss, he can delegate some of his responsibilities to trusted employees and design his own work schedule, allowing himself plenty of time to spend with his family and bike with his friends. Art is pretty damn happy.

BE HAPPY IN YOUR WORK

Getting rich smart means becoming wealthy enough to do whatever you want, whenever you want, and having the time to enjoy it at an age when you still have the most important thing: your health. The smartest route to getting filthy, stinking rich is self-employment. Why? It's the only avenue that puts no limit on the amount of money you can make or the time you can devote toward making it.

Most people forget that there are actually two kinds of wealth: outer and inner. Outer wealth consists of having an excess of money and material possessions: cash, stocks, bonds, real estate, grown-up toys — whatever floats your boat. Inner wealth is different: it isn't related to money at all. Inner wealth is nothing more (and nothing less) than being satisfied with your life, both at and away from the office. Getting rich quick or slow may bring you outer wealth, but only getting rich smart will bring you inner wealth as well.

Getting rich smart is more about a lifestyle than a number in your bank account.

Getting rich smart is more about a lifestyle than a number in your bank account. Those who try to get rich quick live their lives in pursuit of one "big break" after another. Those who spend their best years trying to get rich slow live a controlled existence in which every move is well planned and calculated. Those who get rich smart have the confidence and freedom — and the time — to do whatever they want.

THE BOTTOMLESS POT OF GOLD

One principle keeps Nick GetRichQuick and Joe GetRichSlow from being Art GetRichSmart: they see wealth as a finite resource. In their eyes, the world is divided into shares, with a certain amount of money designated for each person, and that's it. Once that money is gone, there isn't any more to go around. If one person is wealthy, it's because he took more than his share; he took someone else's money. So if Nick GetRichQuick owns stock in Company X, and that stock goes up from $100 to $120, Nick thinks he beat some other guy out of $20. But that's not how it works.

Wealth creation is the magic of capitalism. In effect, you create money out of thin air — it's the fruit of your hard work and creativity. There's no limit to how much money there can be in the world. When you make money, you're doing just that: making money. You're not taking it from someone else; you're creating it from nothing. Getting rich smart exercises the abundance model: there's more than enough to go around, because you can create as much wealth as you're willing to work for. If your mind can conceive it, you can create it.

HERBISM: BEING HAPPY IS EASY ONCE YOU REALIZE THAT YOUR OPPORTUNITIES ARE LIMITED ONLY BY YOUR IMAGINATION.

5

BEING YOUR OWN BOSS

(TAKING THE SELF-EMPLOYMENT PLUNGE)

eing self-employed is the best and fastest way to become filthy, stinking rich. Owning your own business lets you leverage huge profits from a small investment while keeping control of the factors that determine your money's growth.

Some may argue that investing in the stock market offers the same advantages, because you, as the stockholder, decide which stocks to purchase and when to buy or sell. But when you buy stocks you're banking on someone else. That's a fancy way of saying that you're hoping to God that Michael Eisner still knows how to run Disney or that Bill Gates stays at Microsoft. There's not much control here — you're merely speculating on someone else's abilities and the emotional mood swings of Wall Street on any given day.

Buying stocks is a wonderful thing if you do it intelligently **33** with the money you've made from your business, but you'll never get filthy, stinking rich solely from investing in the stock market. You'll get there from your business, and the stocks you buy will help turn your small mountain into a big one.

THE THRILL OF RISK

As an entrepreneur, you rely on no one but yourself. This can be scary, but it can also be the most exhilarating, most rewarding challenge you ever take on. Your skill and know-how alone can turn a few thousand dollars into millions. You can start the smallest and simplest business and turn it into an empire. Every big business started as a small one. Steve Jobs started Apple Computers in his garage. Ray Kroc took one hamburger stand and made McDonald's. The type of business is irrelevant. All that matters is your know-how.

Suppose you start an auto repair business out of your own garage with $400–$500 worth of tools and a little advertising. Once you get a good reputation and a little business, you hire one or two mechanics to work with you. Then, using your established name and good management, you lease a garage with office space and hire a few more mechanics. Eventually, you open a second location in another part of town, then a third,

> **Your skill and know-how alone can turn a few thousand dollars into millions.**

then a fourth. Pretty soon you expand to the next city over, and so on. In a matter of just a few years, you will have transformed a couple of thousand dollars into a business empire with an annual income of millions.

Here in Tucson, two Israeli immigrants opened a small brake repair shop a few years ago, and today they have a chain that grosses over $50 million annually. Now that's filthy, stinking rich! There are 22 million small businesses in this country, all started by people who were someone else's employees before they took the self-employment plunge. Do you think each of

34 those entrepreneurs started with millions of dollars in capital? Of course not! The Israeli car repair moguls started with $2,000 and the grease under their fingernails. It's not a question of capital; it's a question of business smarts.

THE RISK OF THRILLS

Let me be perfectly honest with you: Starting your own business is risky. There's a chance you'll fail. But as we have discussed, the only realistic path to great wealth is self-employment. So what does this mean? It means that to become filthy, stinking rich you have to take risks.

There's no way to make great wealth without taking great financial risk. The stark, cold truth is that risk and reward are directly related. Enormous risk, enormous reward. No risk, no reward. That's the nature of the beast.

There are different kinds of risk. Some are serious, others are not. In the grand scheme of things, the risks you take in starting your own business are minimal. Look at it this way: Risk is like an onion — it has many layers. The outer layers are light and peel away easily; those risks are minor. The closer to the core you get, the more serious the risks become. At the very center of the onion is the risk of death. Nothing we're going to discuss comes close to risking your life, so that's not even a question. Outward from the core are other serious risks, such as losing your family or becoming ill. No such outcome is possible as a result of smart entrepreneurship — "smart" being the operative word here. If you do it the get-rich-smart way, the only real risk posed by starting your own business is the lightest, flakiest, most inconsequential outer layer of the onion: losing money.

> **The stark, cold truth is that risk and reward are directly related. That's the nature of the beast.**

I cannot say this enough: Money is just money. It's not your life or your family. It's paper and ink. That's all it is. If you keep your perspective on who you are and what you value, then financial risk should not threaten you. Much like rejection, risk is not personal. It's just part of becoming successful.

THE ENTREPRENEURIAL MIND-SET

The main thing that separates the wage earners from the self-employed is a little thing I like to call the "entrepreneurial mind-set of movement." Let me explain. Wage earners see starting or expanding a business as a risk; the self-employed see it as movement. Those who are employed by others are just treading water or swimming laps. Those who are out there building something of their own are windsurfing. When you challenge the wind, you have to keep moving, feeling the wind and water, changing direction to catch the best waves. It's riskier, but it's thrilling, and if you're good, you can go fast and far.

If you have a sound business idea, a solid plan to implement it, and the willingness to give it all you've got, then the biggest risk is not acting on your idea. If you move on the idea, yes, there's a chance you'll fail. But if you don't move on the idea, it's 100 percent guaranteed that you will never succeed at all. Ask yourself this: Am I on the path to success? If the answer is no, and if you don't change direction, you will end up exactly where you're headed! You won't get anywhere if you don't act. Which risk is greater?

Don't waste a chance to get out there and do something on your own. Don't put it off, promising that someday you'll do it. "Someday" never comes. "Someday" is either today or never.

HERBISM: IF YOU WANT TO HIT A HOME RUN, YOU'VE GOT TO STEP UP TO THE PLATE.

6
THE GROWN-UP'S BOOGIE MAN

(REJECTION IS NOT THE END OF THE WORLD)

Most adults are relatively mature. They don't pick their noses, they don't throw temper tantrums, and they're not afraid of the dark. But mention the word "rejection," and grown adults will run crying to their mommies faster than you can say "insecurity complex."

Rejection — in one form or another — is part of our everyday lives. Regardless, people seem to be incapable of developing a tolerance for it. The ability to quickly shrug off rejection and move on is the single most important skill of the entrepreneur.

The number one reason most people stay at a job they hate is because they're too petrified to look elsewhere and be rejected. Waking up every morning and going to a job that makes you miserable is the most ridiculous and unnecessary thing in 37 the world, but millions of people do it!

THAT'S LIFE

Regardless of what your current job is — whether you realize it or not — you must deal with rejection in one form or another in every aspect of your work. Being denied a promotion, being rejected by a potential customer, having a current client leave you for your competitor — these are all forms of rejection. Do you enjoy cowering in your cubicle, whimpering in fear of that rejection? Or would you prefer to learn how to deal with the inevitable rejection of the business world in a way that would work to your advantage as a successful, self-employed individual?

How much rejection you incur depends on what kind of business you have: passive or aggressive. Aggressive businesses are those with one-on-one contact, such as selling cars or insurance. These fields have a much higher rejection index than passive businesses, those in which you wait for the customer to come to you, such as a restaurant or a landscaping service. Regardless of which model fits your business, rejection is inevitable. There's nowhere to hide from rejection in the business world, so let's learn to deal with it as best we can.

There's nowhere to hide from rejection in the business world, so let's learn to deal with it as best we can.

Rejection takes many forms. It can be a single, large incidence, like failing to raise the start-up capital for your business or losing your biggest customer. But more often than not, rejection takes its shape in smaller, more frequent instances, such as an uninterested customer, a disloyal employee, or a dip in profits. Don't let the size of the rejection affect you. Regardless of how insignificant or detrimental the failure may be, your mind-set must be "It doesn't bother me." You must decide up

38 front that you're not going to let it upset you, and that's it. Sound a little too easy? Let an old pro show you how.

REJECTION BY THE NUMBERS

Dealing with rejection — of any size or importance — is a simple three-step process. One, two, three, and you're over it and on to more important things. The first step is to acknowledge that rejection is not fun. No sane person enjoys it. I hate it, you hate it, everyone hates it. Don't ever expect to enjoy being rejected. The best we can do is learn to deal with it.

The second step may sound easy, but it tends to be the most difficult for people to perform. You must understand that business rejection is not personal; it's just business. People have a tendency to personalize rejection. It's not a personal insult against you; it's just not the right moment. At a different time or at a different place, under different circumstances, rejection might have been replaced by success. A customer may love your product but be unable to afford it at the moment. A potential investor may believe in your idea but be in a bad mood the day you approach her. Your competitor down the street may be having a sale, pulling customers away from your business. It's not you, it's the culmination of hundreds of circumstances beyond your control.

> **You must understand that business rejection is not personal; it's just business.**

The third step is to do whatever it takes to get through it. Some people listen to motivational tapes or talk to a friend. Others distract themselves with a hobby. Personally, I get amnesia. I am a counter-rejectionary. When somebody rejects me, I figure it's his loss and I forget his name. I honestly believe in projects that I am involved in, so I can honestly say that I think everyone else should be involved, too. If I approach a client or an investor with the opportunity to get involved in a great project and he turns me down, it's his mistake. I put him completely out

of my mind, forget about the rejection, and move on. In order 39
for this philosophy to work, you must have a fundamental belief
in what you're doing. If you're just pursuing your job to make
a quick buck and not because you think it has excellent long-
term potential, you shouldn't be pursuing it at all.

HERBISM: 1. THIS REJECTION THING SUCKS. 2. OH, WELL, IT'S
HIS LOSS. 3. I'M SORRY — WHO ARE YOU AGAIN?

7
LEARN FAST BY SCREWING UP

(MY GREATEST SUCCESS WAS FAILING)

I f life has taught me anything, it's this: If you want to begin with almost nothing and make the big bucks, starting your own business is the best way to do it. Why should you believe me? Because I'm filthy, stinking rich, and because I got there not by earning fancy degrees or inheriting daddy's business (not that there's anything wrong with lucky sperm!), but by learning my lessons the hard way.

And I've learned, in particular, one very simple lesson: Rich people and poor people are exactly the same, except in one respect — rich people think rich. In other words, if all the money on the planet were confiscated and then handed out **41** equally to every person on earth the same day, it wouldn't be long before the rich were rich again, the poor once again poor, and the middle class right back in the middle. So our task in this book is clear: I will teach you to think filthy, stinking rich.

MY LIFE AND HARD TIMES

My story is not very different from a lot of people's. I had a miserable childhood. My parents divorced when I was two; I never saw my natural father alive again. My mother remarried to an abuser, and — well, frankly, it's pretty easy to figure out the rest (don't you just hate to listen to forty-year-old men still whining about their childhood?). I rebelled. I broke with my male family tradition of becoming a professional by dropping out of college in my first year. I joined the Navy, became a Russian linguist, and spent most of the next four years doing all the things I would have done in college — socializing, drinking, and barfing.

I love to stay busy, so late in my Navy career, I started working nights at a local pet store selling dogs, cats, and other little critters on commission. It wasn't long before I was making more money there than in the service. Being twenty, I added two plus two and got five: I figured I was God's gift to pet retailing.

> If all money were confiscated and handed out equally, it wouldn't be long before the rich were rich again and the poor were poor again.

By that time I had married my first wife and we had a daughter. After my discharge, we settled in Loveland, Colorado, where our son was born. It was there that I opened my first business, a pet store. Making every mistake that I'll teach you not to do, I went bankrupt at twenty-one. It was no fun, but now, in 20/20 hindsight, I can see it was my real-life MBA.

So I had to start again from nothing. An accident of fate led me to the life insurance business. Frankly, it was pretty much the only way I could see to support my family in any kind of

42 comfort without a college degree or technical skills. There wasn't much demand for Russian linguists in Loveland at the time.

AN IMPORTANT INSIGHT

As providence would have it, my life insurance career turned out to be a great thing, because it was there that the truth finally dawned on me: I am a great salesman! But although failure had taught me a lot about business, I hadn't learned a bloody thing about life, and I proceeded to destroy my marriage through workaholism. I worked day and night, told myself it was the right thing to do for my family, and effectively forgot what my wife looked like. Predictably, she met someone else and left me — not predictably — alone to raise our two children.

> Although failure had taught me a lot about business, I hadn't learned a bloody thing about life.

Being a single parent with no income (unless I earned a commission) was less fun than going bankrupt, but just as when my business failed, I learned through pain. I promised myself that if I ever got another chance, my watchword would be balance. My career evolved gradually from insurance to investments, and I found I had a talent for picking stocks. Coupling that with my sales skills and business experience brought me a thriving investment practice, managing millions of dollars for hundreds of folks all across the United States, that I still own and run today. Add to that my other business interests in media, car rentals, real estate development, and food service, and, well, self-employment has been very, very good to me!

Along the way my luck held out, and I met and married the greatest woman who has ever lived, my wife, Terri. Now with a total of four great kids, we are living our dreams. I can truly say that I want for nothing. But it was failure that made it all possible, and remembering that pain makes me appreciate how sweet success really is.

Let's be honest. If you were already filthy, stinking rich, you probably wouldn't be reading this book. My point in telling you my story is not to prove how cool I am, but to help you understand that you and I are very much alike. Life has thrown us both a curveball or two. But I've learned to see them coming and hit them. And when we're done with our journey through this book, you'll know how, too!

HERBISM: ADVICE IS ONLY AS GOOD AS ITS SOURCE. WHOSE ADVICE ARE YOU TAKING?

PART II

CHOOSE YOUR FUTURE

(Planning Your Arrival)

8
THE THREE BUSINESS IDEAS

(CATCH YOUR WAVE AND RIDE IT)

You've decided to start your own business, and you're rarin' to go! But what's it going to be? There are millions of business ideas out there to choose from, and you can become filthy, stinking rich from any number of them. Deciding which of your ideas is a winner isn't as tricky as it seems because, believe it or not, they all fall into one of three categories: original, just plain aggressive, or niche-fillers.

INVENT SOMETHING

The only truly original business ideas are new inventions. If you've invented something that no one else has ever thought of before, great. That's a hot business idea. Hire a good lawyer, patent that sucker, get it on the market, and let the royalties come pouring into your bank account. But beware!

48 If you're like most inventors, you're great at creating things, but you're probably not that good at making money. So find a partner or manager you can trust to run the business end of it for you, or sell the idea to a big company for a mountain of money, like Bette Graham did after she invented Liquid Paper. On the other hand, maybe you're another Thomas Edison or Alexander Graham Bell and can start and run your own industry.

> If you're like most inventors, you're probably not that good at making money — so find a partner or manager you can trust to run your business.

People tend to go through life believing that you have to think up a new, original, ground-breaking idea in order to make it big. It's not true. You can take an existing concept and come up with a better way of doing it.

OLD IDEAS, NEW APPROACHES

That brings us to just plain aggressive ideas, which include the majority of all successful businesses. Aggressive ideas take an existing product and deliver it to the public in some improved way. They are considered aggressive because dozens — if not hundreds — of other companies are trying to deliver the same product with a different twist.

Fast-food hamburger chains are a perfect example. McDonald's, Burger King, Wendy's — God knows none of them invented the hamburger. They were, however, smart enough to take a really common product that was widely accepted by the masses and deliver it to them in a standardized fashion. How do they compete? Each chain has its own little twist that makes it slightly different from the next. But each always — without fail — delivers the product in its own standard way.

Ta-daa! Business genius. Before McDonald's, there was no such thing as a national hamburger chain. Ray Kroc created an entirely new industry based on a product that had been around for decades. Every time you stop at a McDonald's, regardless of where you are, you know it's going to be clean, fast, and cheap.

They are not the world's greatest hamburgers by any stretch of 49 the imagination, but they are the world's cleanest, fastest, cheapest, best-known hamburgers.

E-commerce, selling on the Internet, is the latest just-plain-aggressive idea. There are millions of stores selling books, but when Jeff Bezos started selling them online at Amazon.com, that was aggressive. Now he's a billionaire and on the cover of *Time* magazine.

More often than not, it's better to be the aggressor than the originator. Inventing a product and delivering it to the masses are two different talents. Just because you think of it doesn't mean you'll make money doing it. Have you ever heard of Richard Dudgeon? William Burton? Philo T. Farnsworth? No? I'm not surprised. They invented the automobile, gasoline, and television, respectively. Those products, like most products,

> More often than not, it's better to be the aggressor than the originator. Inventing a product and delivering it to the masses are two different talents.

were invented by people whose talent was inventing, not business. It took the business savvy of Henry Ford, John D. Rockefeller, and David Sarnoff to bring those business ideas to life. Business success is all in the delivery. It's not what product or service you sell that matters, it's how you do it. Instead of inventing something new, you will most likely become filthy, stinking rich by taking a product or service that already exists and delivering it to the public in a new or better way.

PROVEN SOLUTIONS FOR NEW NEEDS

Finally, we have "niche-fillers." These are businesses that are neither original nor particularly different in how they deliver their product or service. They simply fill an existing need in an established marketplace.

The advantage of starting a niche-filler business is that you don't have to invent anything new. You know your product or service has found acceptance elsewhere. Most of the mistakes

50 you can make have already been made, so you can learn how to run the business before you run it.

Let's look at a new business idea of mine to see how this works in the real world. Mexico is just an hour's flight from Tucson, and I often fly there in my plane. While vacationing there on weekends with my family, I saw other travelers from Arizona, many of them driving down to Mexico to scuba dive. The problem for the scuba divers, however, was that the drive took a big five- or six-hour chunk of diving time, each way, out of their weekends.

I saw a need. Then I figured out how to fill it: an air taxi service for scuba diving groups, flying from Tucson to Rocky Point and San Carlos, Mexico, both prime diving spots. It seemed an excellent idea from the start — a market that no one else was exploiting.

Great ideas are much easier to evaluate when you have a set of criteria you can apply to them. When considering a new business opportunity, I ask myself four questions (I call them the "Fab Four" because they usually attract gold or platinum):

1. Does the product or service have mass acceptance?

2. Is the existing competition somehow missing the boat?

3. Can I deliver the product or service cheaper, better, or faster?

4. Is there enough profit to generate big rewards?

I examined my air taxi idea in the light of these four questions. Here are the answers I came up with:

1. Mass acceptance? There are three dive shops in Tucson, one in San Carlos, and two in Rocky Point, all doing as much business as they can handle. To that, add fishermen and locals in Mexico who need to get to Tucson for business and personal reasons. Yes, the acceptance is there.

2. Competition? America West is the only airline that flies to San Carlos. You have to backtrack from Tucson to Phoenix first (a trip 120 miles in the wrong direction), spend $320 plus tax, and the trip takes three hours forty-five minutes! There are no flights to Rocky Point. Yep, the gap is there.

3. Cheaper, better, faster? I can operate my aircraft, a brand-new turboprop with leather seats, air conditioning, and

CD stereo, for $300 per hour, making my total out-of-pocket expense $600 round trip. The plane seats nine passengers. I can fill three seats at $200 each round trip and break even. Every seat after that is gravy! Plus, I shorten the trip by two hours and forty-five minutes.

4. Profit potential? I called all the dive shops in Tucson, San Carlos, and Rocky Point, plus local travel agents, fishing boats, and tour operators. According to the amount of business they see every day, we ought to have no problem filling the seats. At six seats filled for one trip daily (that's only two-thirds capacity), I stand to net over $100,000 per plane per year. Not bad for a part-time business!

An air-taxi service is not a new invention. It's not even an aggressive take on an already existing concept. Nonetheless, it is a business that satisfies the four questions, and no one else either thought of creating an air-taxi service from Tucson to Mexico or knew how to raise the capital to do it. It is a very specific niche that needed to be filled. Such a business idea has just as much potential for making you big money as an original or aggressive idea.

OPPORTUNITY ROCKS

Every business has to have its edge to gain and keep as many customers as possible. Either come up with an original idea of your own, or take a fresh twist on a business that already exists, or find a need and fill it. Once you've conceived of an idea with potential, apply the four questions. If they can all be answered favorably, you've got yourself a strong basis for building a successful business.

HERBISM: THE WHEEL WAS A GOOD INVENTION, BUT THE TIRE WAS MORE PROFITABLE. FIND A NEED, FILL IT, AND GET RICH!

9

HAVING FUN CAN BE PROFITABLE

(BE HAPPY IN YOUR WORK)

This is a short, sweet little slice of advice that may go without saying, but I'm going to say it anyway: When deciding on a business, use what God gave you. This ought to be obvious, but to a lot of people, it's not.

The basic premise of this approach is understanding that everyone has multiple talents. However, different people have different talents. And just as every person is different from the next, so is each business. Every type of business is suited for a certain type of person with certain talents.

I can't tell you how many times I've seen people force themselves into businesses or industries that do not suit them! It's the most easily avoided of all business mistakes. All you need to do is take a look in the mirror. Think back over your accomplishments and failures. What are you good at? What do you suck at?

If working with people tends to get on your nerves, outside sales should not be involved in your business in any way, shape, or form. Mail order or the Internet might be more up your alley. If you're a real people person, don't get stuck behind a desk, staring at a computer screen all day. If you feel trapped in an office, pick a business that lets you travel around town.

The possibilities are endless. Don't frustrate yourself and waste your energy trying to cram a square peg into a round hole. Pay attention to yourself. Recognize your skills. Be aware of your weaknesses. But most important, know how to have fun.

It doesn't have to be an obviously fun thing — most businesses are not walking, talking parties. But you do have to choose a career that you like, or one that at least has an aspect that you like. Open a store or begin a service that involves an activity that you enjoy. You're going to spend quite a lot of time developing and running your business, so you might as well have some fun while you're at it.

> Don't frustrate yourself and waste your energy trying to cram a square peg into a round hole.

A couple of words to the wise: Never, ever go into business in an area you know nothing about. Stick to what you know like the back of your hand. That's just common sense. Beware also of doing something you love just because you love it. Make a business plan and see if there's money in it. If I had known these things when I opened my first business, I could have saved myself a lot of grief!

HERBISM: YOU'LL MAKE A LOT MORE MONEY EXPLOITING THE TALENTS YOU HAVE THAN TRYING TO DEVELOP NEW ONES.

10
DRAW YOUR OWN ROAD MAP

(SHARING YOUR DREAM)

Now that you've decided what business you're starting, in order to implement it, you need to write a business plan. This little number is going to be the basis for raising your start-up capital, as well as a reference for gauging the success of your business.

A business plan covers every issue, contingency, and number that relates to your business — everything a potential investor has to know. In its simplest form, it covers three areas:

1. **Idea:** the basic concept of your business — the product or service you propose to sell.

2. **Market:** who's going to buy your product or service, and how you're going to persuade them to do so.

3. **Profit potential:** revenue, cost, and profit projections, **55** including such data as what it's going to cost to set up your business, your estimated operating expenses, and how much money you expect to net after that glorious day in the not-too-distant future when you reach the break-even point.

This is the document you're going to use to persuade people to invest money in your dream. The profit/loss numbers are the most important; they will bolster your case when you present the plan to potential investors. But almost as important is what's up front — your brilliant business idea. Here's where you have to grab their attention and make your best case.

BELIEVE IN YOURSELF

Imagine you have just five minutes alone with a millionaire. What would you say to persuade him or her to invest in you and your business? That's what you put in the first two parts of your plan — the idea and the market. Explain precisely what product or service you're going to offer and how your delivery will be superior to all others'. You believe your business is unique and special, don't you? Convey that confidence in the proposal, and pass it on to the investors.

Don't be afraid to sing your own praises. If you don't, no one else will.

Discuss the competition openly and straightforwardly. Everyone knows you'll have competition; if you don't mention it, you'll look like an idiot. Explain with confidence how you think your competitors are missing the boat and how you plan to exploit their weaknesses.

List your qualifications, and don't be shy. Play to your strengths. Don't be afraid to be effusive as long as you're being honest. If you're very good at something, why pretend you're not? You can be honest without being arrogant. It's not bragging. It doesn't make you God's gift to humanity. Everyone is good at something, and if your talents are going to help the

56 business prosper, let 'em rip! Don't be afraid to sing your own praises. If you don't, no one else will. Believe me, your competition is not going to line up to sing 'em for you!

GIVE IT TO 'EM STRAIGHT

Two points of advice: First, give the bad news up front. I've always found, when preparing and presenting a business proposal, that it's best to get the searing pain out of the way immediately. High-rolling investors tend to be very keen businesspeople. Just as everyone knows about competition, everyone knows failure is possible. If you pretend it's not, you'll look inexperienced and foolish. It will add enormous credibility to your proposal if you openly admit, right off the bat, that you may all lose your money.

Second, make sure this is a well-written document. If you don't write well, find someone who does. You get only one chance at a first impression, and no one is going to invest money in someone with the grammar skills of a second-grader. No one may ever notice or mention that your proposal is well written, but it's a subliminal quality that engenders confidence. Remember, too, that this is not Scrabble, so forget the four-syllable, fifty-point words. Most people speak and think in plain old five- or ten-point words. If this business idea is a gold mine, say it! "We're going to make big bucks, people!" Not "I think we stand to accumulate net profits in excess of the average business venture of this variety." There's no need to be pompous. If your business idea is really that phenomenal, you don't need to dress it up in fancy language.

HERBISM: **FORGET ABOUT POLITENESS, PRETENSION, AND POLITICAL CORRECTNESS. SAY WHAT'S ON YOUR MIND!**

11
THE MAGIC BUDGET

(MONEY COMES AND MONEY GOES)

So far, so good. You've created a first part for your business plan that would no doubt make Donald Trump sit up and take notice, and your prospective investors will be

perched on the edges of their chairs in anticipation. Now it's time for the rubber to meet the road. You've got to crunch some numbers.

Of course, you're not working up a budget just to impress investors. You're doing it to give yourself the best possible chance to succeed. There's no such thing as too much cash in a small business. There is, however, such a thing as not enough cash, and that's why accurate budget projections are so important. A well-conceived budget will empower your business to absorb any and all unforeseen expenses. And — should your business go south later — the numbers had better be there.

FOUR FUNDAMENTALS

Let's start by explaining the four buzz words of this chapter: budget, revenue, profit, and loss. Your budget is an estimate of how much money it will take to operate your business, including all the expenses outlined in your business plan. When projecting your budget, assume zero sales. That's right — assume that your business will not bring in a single nickel the first year.

Next, add up your estimated expenses for the first year. Put a number on everything you can think of: how much inventory you'll need and what it will cost; square feet of office space needed and rental cost; monthly utilities; the number of employees and how much you're going to pay them; insurance, taxes, interest, licenses, fees — everything that can possibly cost you money. Double that figure. Add in the cost of fixtures, signs, and business equipment. Now that's the amount of start-up capital you need to raise from investors. If your estimated monthly expenses total $10,000, that's $120,000 for one year of sales-free operation. So you need to raise at least $240,000.

Once you open your doors and hang out your sign, you're going to run into a million unexpected things that you cannot possibly plan for.

Why twice the amount of actual cost? To be realistic! There's no way you can accurately predict how much money you'll really need. The $10,000-per-month figure is what I like to call a SWAG, or scientific wild-ass guess. In other words, there's only so much you can predict. Once you open your doors and hang out your sign, you're going to run into a million unexpected things that you cannot possibly plan for. Each of these occurrences is going to increase your costs in some way.

You have to double your projected budget to compensate for the "what-ifs." "What if my advertising isn't effective? What if I need to hire more employees? What if I need to improve the quality of my product or service? What if I've drastically underestimated the cost of utilities?" What if, what if, what if! You can have the most wonderfully efficient business plan in the world, but there's no way to plan for "what-ifs" — except to have double the necessary cash stashed away, ready whenever you need it. Whether you use it or not, just think how much better you'll sleep knowing you have twice as much money as you need, available at a moment's notice.

Now for those other three buzz words: revenue, profit, and loss. Revenue is gross income, the total amount your business brings in. Profit is what's left after you've paid your expenses (including taxes), and loss is when your revenue is less than your expenses. Let's go back to the example of the business with monthly expenses of $10,000. If your revenue is $10,000, you break even. If your revenue is $12,000, you make $2,000 profit. If your revenue is $8,000, your loss is $2,000. Pretty simple concepts, no?

When projecting revenue, profit, and loss, keep your estimates modest. It's always best to overestimate expenses and underestimate profit. In fact, the safest way to do this is to project three sets of numbers for each: best case, worst case, and most probable case. The worst-case scenario assumes zero sales. You have enough cash (this is what the budget is for!) to pay for all business-related expenses, but you're not making any profit. Now this is not a very realistic situation, but it is possible. The most-probable-case scenario is the most realistic of the three estimates, with moderate sales and slow but steady growth. The best-case scenario is a nice dream that will help you sleep through the inevitable restless nights ahead.

YOU'RE ON YOUR OWN

While trying to project your three sets of numbers, you may be wondering, especially if you're a first-time entrepreneur, how you are expected to know what "moderate sales" and "slow but steady growth" mean in terms of your business. Well, you're not! You have to go find out. This is not an industry-specific book, and I cannot possibly include estimates for every type of business. But fear not! The resources from which you can draw this information are endless. Within every industry are organizations and associations that

60   tabulate and publish this boring but necessary data. Check out the bookstore or your local library. Books, magazines, journals, and of course the Internet — there are mountains of information out there, just waiting to be found.

CAUTION: LAWYERS AHEAD

Not only will having three sets of numbers guide you through those first tough months, but it will help forestall legal action by pissed-off investors if your business fails. Include in your business plan best, worst, and most-probable-case scenarios for the business's outcome, as well as the worst worst-case scenario: failure. We've already discussed how mentioning the possibility of failure will add credibility to your proposal, but it will also help keep you safe as a kitten in the land of legality. If investors are told beforehand that there is no guarantee of profit or even return of initial investment, they cannot realistically take legal action claiming otherwise.

Sometimes realism has nothing to do with it; that's why God made lawyers.

Of course, sometimes realism has nothing to do with it; that's why God made lawyers. Get help from the pros early in your business planning. Find an accountant who specializes in small businesses, especially your kind of business, and who can alert you to financial pitfalls and head off potential tax problems. And get yourself a good lawyer — again, a specialist — who can keep you from stumbling into legal quicksand. Ask around among your fellow small business owners; get a referral from someone who's filthy rich and happy.

COMPUTER MAGIC

There are two ways to write the numbers part of your business plan: the long, boring, painful, old-fashioned way, or the quick and easy way. If you've been paying any attention at all, you know that I like to get out of the office and enjoy the good life. That's why I recommend putting away 61 the quill pen and abacus and using business-planning software.

There are at least a dozen different programs on the market that require you to do nothing more than input the numbers. Then the programs do their whizzing and whirling, and whammo! They generate amazingly accurate and unbelievably fast business plans that will make your head spin. I've sat and fiddled with almost all of them, and there's not one that's significantly better than another. With the same data entered, they all generated figures within pennies of each other. The only difference between them is which colors the pretty little graphs are drawn in; they all look good when you plug them into the plan you've whipped out using your word processing software.

The software will prompt you: "How much is your monthly rent? How much is your quarterly marketing budget?" To help your software do its magic, you need to have some idea of what you're doing. Do some preliminary research. Ask around town. Check out the Web. Compare with other businesses like the one you want to open. Have numbers ready to plug into the software. If you get to a question you can't answer, just stop what you're doing and go find out. It's really very simple and very user-friendly. Assuming you're willing to do the research, you can easily write a business plan using this software.

GET READY TO FLEX

A word of warning: Once you've completed all of the software's questions, you're going to have this beautiful, computer-generated, whiz-bang business plan, complete with charts, graphs, buttons, and whistles. You're going to be very proud of yourself and very excited. You will most likely fall deeply in love with your marvelous new business plan. It's wonderful, I know. But this business plan is not the gospel. It is not etched in stone, and it is not the final word on your business's future. It's a starting point.

There are really only two alternatives for how this will all turn out: better than you planned, or worse. But I absolutely

62 guarantee you that it will never, ever turn out exactly the way you expected. Business plans and their writers are powerful only if they are flexible. If something within your business plan doesn't work out as well as you predicted, ask yourself why. Reexamine the situation and see what you can do different. Or maybe things will work out better than you planned, in which case you should examine your business plan and try to figure out what caused things to go so well — then keep doing it. The point is, don't be afraid to change your business plan as you go along. Let it adjust to the movement of your business.

> Your business plan is not the gospel. It is not etched in stone, and it is not the final word on your business's future. It's a starting point.

Don't stick with the plan just because that's what you said you were going to do. It's just a piece of paper. It's not going to get its feelings hurt if you change it.

HERBISM: MEN PLAN AND GOD LAUGHS. MAKE A PLAN, BUT BE PREPARED TO PIVOT.

12
CUSTOM-BUILD YOUR EMPIRE

(A NOTE ON BUSINESS STRUCTURE)

So you've drawn up your business plan and you're ready to go — almost. What about the structure of your business? For legal and tax reasons, there are four basic choices: sole proprietorships, partnerships, corporations, and LLCs. They all set out to do the same thing — run smoothly and turn over a nice chunk of profit — but with different degrees of freedom and protection. Which is best for you?

SOLE PROPRIETORSHIP: RISKY BUSINESS

A sole proprietorship is a person doing business without any legal structure, form, or protection. In other words, it's just a fancy way of saying, "I'm going to call myself by a business name, but really it's just me." You can call it

64 "Herb's Ice Cream Shop," but in actuality it's just little old Herb selling ice cream. You file your income taxes under your own social security number, and that's it.

A sole proprietorship is the quickest and easiest business structure to establish. There's no paperwork, no legal battles, and the start-up cost can be close to nothing. You can conceptualize a business at breakfast and be in business by lunchtime without ever having to wheel and deal with partners or committees. You can do what you want, when you want, without any hassles. That's the upside.

> In a sole proprietorship, you are personally liable. If the company gets sued, you get sued personally.

The downside, however, is substantial. A sole proprietorship gives you absolutely no legal protection. Zero. Zilch. Nada. If a customer at Herb's Ice Cream Shop slips on a wet floor, breaks her back, and sues the shop, who really gets sued? That's right — Herb. In a sole proprietorship, you are personally liable. If the company gets sued, you get sued personally. If the company doesn't pay its taxes, the IRS comes after you personally. It's going to be your house, your car, and your kids' college funds going down the tube. That's an unnecessary risk.

PARTNERSHIP: SINKING SHIP

Partnerships function exactly like sole proprietorships. The only difference is the number of people. Often people see partnerships as a union of just two businesspeople, but a partnership can consist of any number of partners — two, three, four, it makes no difference.

Much like sole proprietorships, partnerships are relatively easy and inexpensive to establish and run. Although I don't encourage partnerships, if you do go that route, I highly recommend getting with an attorney first to draw up a partnership agreement. Other than that, there's hardly any paperwork or legalese involved. Unfortunately, just like sole proprietorships, partnerships do not provide you with a single shred of legal protection. They also have the enormous added problem of personality conflict. I have witnessed the rise and fall of hundreds of partners — most of whom started out as good friends. Partnerships that have survived basic commercial and legal risks have dissolved solely because of personality conflict. Believe me, almost every partner will sooner or later think, "I do all the work, and my partner's a lazy bum!" My advice on partnerships: Forget it! But if you insist on forming one, at least draw up the business equivalent of a pre-nup: a buy/sell agreement. This protects both of you if either decides to bail out. You'll have the option of buying your partner out, rather than putting up with anyone your partner wants to sell to, and you'll have some assurance that the price and terms are right.

CORPORATION: A WEB OF RED TAPE

A corporation is a fictional being that exists solely in the world of legality — a puppet you use to perform all your business transactions. That's not really you writing that check, ordering inventory, signing the lease; it's the corporation.

The big plus to all this puppet talk is the legal protection it provides. Someone can sue the corporation and win, but the corporation is only a fictional being. Whoever sues the corporation wins a lawsuit against air. As long as the corporation exists, it acts as a shield — the "corporate veil" — protecting you personally from any legal liability. The corporation takes all the body blows for you.

> The corporation acts as a shield, protecting you personally from any legal liability. It takes all the body blows for you.

What's the catch? Well, it's twofold. First, there are a million little legal dos and don'ts to setting up and running a corporation. Therefore, you need to work in depth with an attorney to make sure you establish your corporation correctly — an expensive, time-consuming process.

Second, you must follow to the letter the rules that define a corporation; otherwise the protection it normally affords you

66   is annulled. And man, oh man, are there tons of rules! Board meetings, minutes, shareholders, reports — the list goes on and on. More often than not, members of a corporation cannot keep up with all the nonsense legalese, and they unwittingly pierce their own corporate veil — something plaintiffs' lawyers love to allege. Then, when push comes to shove, all they're left with is an expensive, legalistic, pain-in-the-butt corporation that gives them a giant headache but no protection! And for a lot of new ventures, creditors require your personal guarantee anyway, making the whole protection concept moot. No, thank you.

LLC: THE EIGHTH WONDER OF THE WORLD

A limited-liability company is based on the same puppet concept as a corporation, only without all the formalities and red tape. It's the best of both worlds: freedom and protection. Essentially, an LLC is a partnership that acts like a corporation. The head honcho is called the "managing partner," everyone else is a "member," and all are shielded from liability by the LLC. Furthermore, an LLC can take advantage of all the retirement plan and employee benefits of a traditional corporation.

An LLC is almost as easy to set up and maintain as a sole proprietorship or a partnership. The only legal requirements are the initial meeting with a lawyer, to draw up the paperwork, and the annual filing of the company's tax return. That's it. And then off you go to do things that are actually fun! No minutes, no committees, no nothing. Pretty simple, eh? Plus, an LLC is even more protective than a corporation, but with none of that complicated corporate red tape to risk forgetting. Boy, do I love these things!

HERBISM: FORGET THE PARTNERS AND THE CORPORATE HEADACHES! AN LLC IS THE ONLY WAY TO GO.

13
WHERE THE MONEY HIDES

(...AND WHERE IT DOESN'T)

Now that you've drawn up your business plan, designed your business structure, and fine-tuned your business proposal to attract the attention of smart backers, all you need to get the ball rolling is the start-up capital.

BEWARE THE BANK

You should have a good idea of how much cash you need based on the projected budget in your business plan. Now, you probably don't have the money gathering dust in your bank account, or you wouldn't be reading this chapter. This means you're going to have to get the money elsewhere. You need to get together with some venture capitalists.

68 First I'll tell you where you're not going to get it. You're not going to get it from the bank. Bankers are not, by nature, venture capitalists. The bank will only lend you money based on your assets. If you need the money to start a business, then you obviously can't use the business as collateral, which means the bank won't give you any money to acquire what they consider the assets necessary to be granted the loan. Dizzying, isn't it? Banks definitely have their place in the grand scheme of things. Down the road, once your business is established and stable, banks are a wonderful place to go for expansion loans or loans to smooth out the peaks and valleys of an established cash flow. But for getting your business off the ground, you need to look elsewhere.

> **Banks are fine for expansion loans, but for getting your business off the ground, look elsewhere.**

FORGET THE FAMILY

The second place not to get the money is family. You may think that if your family has the money, why not ask them for it, but interfamily loans are a big no-no. First of all, it's hard to get your family to take you seriously. Just because they love you doesn't necessarily mean they will feel comfortable forking over their life savings to you. You may think your family considers you mature and responsible, but that's when you're dealing with someone else's money. In my family, for example, I will be Little Herby forever. Regardless of how successful I become, my family still pinches my cheeks and sees me as an eight-year-old. And that's the way it is in most families.

Another problem with raising capital from your family is that you cannot risk bankrupting them. If you raise money from a total stranger and go bankrupt, it's ugly, but it's not maiming. If you bankrupt a family member, you're screwed for life. You think loan sharks are harsh? Wait until you blow Aunt Ethel's retirement fund. Every Thanksgiving and every Christmas and every Hanukkah and every New Year's and every Groundhog Day for the rest of your life — you'll never hear the end of it. You'll never live it down. You can become a billionaire later and pay old Aunt Ethel back ten times over, but she'll never let you forget how you lost the $20,000 that took her thirty-five years to scrimp and save. If you're going to approach your family for capital, you have to have a foolproof, 100 percent guaranteed business plan — and there's no such thing.

There's one exception to the rule against using family money: a gift or advance on inheritance from your parents. Since this kind of gift need never be repaid, nobody but you gets hurt if you lose it.

SHUN THE SERVICE CLUB

Third, when looking for potential investors, don't waste your time at the local service club, whether Kiwanis, Lions, Optimist, Rotary, or other. For the most part, those clubs are a bunch of salespeople selling to each other. I know they do a lot of good work for the community, and I have nothing against them. But the reality is that people with big-time money do not, with rare exceptions, hang out at community service clubs. If you want to join them to get your name out there once your business is up and running, fabulous idea. But as far as initial investors are concerned, if you're looking to your local service club for help, you're barking up the wrong tree.

ON YOUR MARK . . .

Now that I've said where *not* to look for start-up capital, let me tell you where you *can* look. You're going to have to raise the money from rich people who are, at the beginning, total strangers to you. But no one in his right mind is going to hand over a wad of cash to a complete stranger. You have to develop relationships. How, you might ask, do I develop relationships with people I don't even know? Simple. You hang out where rich people hang out.

70 Here's a short list of ideas to consider:

1. Your church, temple, or mosque.

2. Your kid's sports team. Volunteer to coach a Little League team. Rich guys dote on their kids.

3. Local politics. This generally works only if you are a conservative or live in a large city such as Los Angeles or New York.

4. Charities and fund-raising. This is the best place to meet rich guys' wives!

5. The "right" health club. This must be in the best section of town, and you must be in seriously good shape.

There's no one place that will do it for you. Be inventive. Out here in Tucson the absolute best place to start is the old, local country club. The bad news is that, to afford the entry fee, you may have to do without food or electricity for a while. The good news is that most country clubs offer junior or associate memberships. In Tucson, the most established country club has a $30,000 initiation fee, but this fee is waived until you reach the age of thirty-five. You can join, pay a monthly fee as a junior member, then jump it up later. If you can possibly, in any way, shape, or form, get into a country club environment, I highly recommend that you do so.

Put yourself into a nonwork environment where wealthy people hang out.

Here's what you do. Start showing up at the club and get thrown into a golf foursome. (Important tip: Take golf lessons and get good!) You never know who you're going to end up playing golf with. It doesn't matter — the other three players will all have more money than you.

Actually, you don't have to join a country club. Just put yourself into a nonwork environment where wealthy people hang out. Everybody has hobbies, especially rich people. Get involved in tennis, fly-fishing, sailing, flying. That's where you'll meet rich people. Be logical; if you were filthy, stinking rich, what kind of hobbies would you pursue — a brewsky with the boys down at the bowling alley, or a cocktail on the 19th hole?

GET SET . . .

Once you find yourself in the country club (or on the tennis court, or knee deep in a trout stream), do not, under any circumstances, talk about money. You're the new guy or girl. The established members are naturally going to be suspicious of you at first. Bringing up the subject of money with them would be business suicide. Of course, what you're secretly saying to yourself as you wet your pants is, "Oh my God, I'm playing golf with the rich guys!" But you have to be nonchalant.

If the subject of money comes up, jokingly avoid it. When I was first starting out and people asked me what I did for a living, I would never answer seriously; the fact that I managed money would have immediately put them on guard. I would say, "I'm in organized crime." And they'd laugh and say, "No, really. What do you do?" "I'm a professional golfer." Now, if you had been on the golf course with me then, you'd know just how funny that is. Put them at ease. If they really want to know about your career, make them pry it out of you!

You have to be patient. Take your time; build your relationship. I don't mean days; I mean months. A year, maybe. Would you give a large sum of money to some guy you've played golf with two or three times? Of course not! You have to establish trust. The time it takes to do this is exactly why, once you have a great business idea, you need to act on it immediately. As soon as you think of a workable idea, begin looking for potential investors. While you're

The quickest way to piss off a person is to make a promise you have no intention of keeping.

taking the time to gain their friendship and trust, you can be drawing up a solid, realistic business plan to show them — when the time is right.

But the time isn't right yet. First you need to ingratiate yourself with the group. How? The best way is to do a lot of selfless things and follow through on what you say you'll do, every time. The quickest way to piss off a person is to make a

72   promise you have no intention of keeping. So if John Rich Guy offhandedly mentions to you that he needs something, and you have a connection that may help him get it, then get it for him, no matter what lengths you have to go to. Take advantage of any opportunity to help a rich person.

Keep in mind that anything you do for John Rich Guy is a favor; it's free. When he tries to thank you by giving you something in return, turn it down. No matter what. Don't take money, don't take gifts, don't take gratuities, don't take anything. If he insists, just say something like, "Don't worry about it. Friends help friends." You're trying to establish credibility. You need to be unbelievably decent, unbelievably honest, unbelievably straight, someone who never, ever takes money for a favor.

So if you sell cars and you can get one of these potential investors the car his kid wants at invoice, do it. Don't take a single nickel on the markup. If he's thrilled that you were able to help him get it and wants to give you a couple of hundred bucks' worth of gratitude, you tell him, "Nah, we're friends. I'd feel stupid taking money from you."

If a potential investor mentions that she and her husband would like to go out of town and get away for a weekend and you know they have a couple of kids, volunteer to watch them. Whatever you can do for them, do it. But never, ever profit from these people early in your relationship.

You need to be as honest as possible about your history. Got something embarrassing in your background? Don't be ashamed. We all do. Bring it out in the course of friendship. It is far better to tell them yourself than to have it come slithering out from under a rock somewhere down the road. Did you go broke in the pet store business when you were twenty-one? Confess. Flunked out of college? Don't manufacture a degree. You were a screwed-up drug addict who turned your life around through Buddha? Tell them. If you get out ahead of it, you can wear it as a badge of honor. They will respect you if you are honest and willing to admit your mistakes, because they've made them, too. You want them to feel completely at ease and safe in your presence.

GO FOR IT!

All right, you've been patient. You've behaved yourself long enough. Now you can begin to reap the rewards. Once you've become friendly with these people and they've deemed you trustworthy, the transition is so easy that it's almost invisible. In the course of conversation, turn to your new rich friend and say, "Bob, I've put together this great business plan. I hate to bother you with it, but I need to raise money for it and I was wondering if you could suggest the right people to talk to. Would you mind reading it and giving me any helpful hints? I would really appreciate your input because you're successful, and I only want to take advice from successful people."

Rich Friend Bob will be more than happy to help you out, since you've been such a good friend and helped him whenever you could. Remember that Rich Friend Bob is rich for a reason: he's a good businessperson. If you've really got a solid business plan with potential, Bob's going to jump at the chance to invest. And even if it's not the right time for Bob, you can bet the farm that Bob will know who to refer you to.

It sounds obvious. It is. Filthy, stinking rich is easy. All it takes is a little initiative and a little common sense. No one is going to make your success happen except you. So get out there and get started!

HERBISM: THE MONEY YOU NEED IS ALL AROUND YOU, HIDING IN PLAIN SIGHT.

14
CASH, PLEASE, AND NO STRINGS

(DON'T PROMISE DOM PERIGNON IF RIPPLE WILL DO)

When you're out there raising money from rich people, there are a couple of important points to keep in mind. First, you may have wondered where

you'll find the time to get the project rolling: "How can I still earn a living, reach my goals, and do it in less than a hundred years?" Second, "What do I have to offer the folks who invest money in my business, above and beyond my good looks?"

BORROWING TIME

Let's start with the first question. Okay, so you want to join the country club and do all this networking, but — oh, baby! — this is going to take more time than you ever expected. And if you're down the road of life a bit and have a family already, this may be time you can ill afford. So let me teach you a possible shortcut: use a center of influence.

What's a center of influence? Well, let's say you have a great business concept, you've done all the requisite business proposals, and everything looks super. Concentrate your networking on successful people you already know who know lots of other successful people just like themselves, and their enthusiasm for your project will save you a lot of time and effort.

There are lots of examples of these folks: successful lawyers with rich clients (perhaps the one who helped you draw up your business documents!), accountants, doctors who love to share great ideas with other docs, heavy-hitter life insurance or real estate agents (make sure they really are big-time and not just legends in their own minds), and last but not least,

People who ask for money are probably people you shouldn't be involved with.

the well-connected folks who know everybody. Just one of these golden people falling in love with your new business idea can make you — and save you a ton of time.

One note of caution. Offer no financial inducement or finder's fee for their help. This is just a subtle form of corruption, a slippery slope that you don't want to start down. Furthermore, people who ask for money are people you probably shouldn't be involved with. If, after the money is raised, you wish to offer them extra stock options or similar rewards for their help, this is perfectly okay. Avoid licensed stockbrokers and financial planners as money sources. They are forbidden to help you by both their codes of ethics and their regulations.

REWARDING INVESTORS

Now, how much security will you have to offer to raise money? As little as you can. You see, if you already have any assets, you need to protect them as much as possible. Investors and, later down the road, bankers will try to get as much security as possible for their investments. This could

76 include a lien on your house, bank accounts, insurance policies, brokerage accounts, etc. Don't offer unless asked, and when asked, divulge only as much as necessary.

Look, these folks are wonderful for helping you with your project, and you're going to reward them with stock or a percentage of the business, as well as interest on the amount they invest. However, they must understand the nature of your venture, including the risk of losing all of their investment. The original shareholders in a big success are always bigger winners than later participants. Just ask Bill Gates and his original crew versus the current shareholders of Microsoft. The current stockholders are doing very well, but nowhere near as well as the early investors. When it comes to venture capital, it's no guts, no glory. If an investor wants any other security for her investment, you might want to reassess whether she's really a good prospect for your venture.

> The original shareholders in a big success are always bigger winners than later participants. Just ask Bill Gates and his original crew versus the current shareholders of Microsoft.

Finally, if you do have to pledge some of your assets as security, okay, but offer only enough to cover the debt — not a penny more. If you're borrowing $25,000 and the equity in your home is $50,000, don't pledge it all. Banks in particular love to get many times their debt covered as security. It looks great on their balance sheet, but it makes a mess of yours! This is why, even if you have assets to use as collateral, banks are out. You can use banks down the road, after you're a big success. Don't offer too much; shop around for a banker who "gets it."

STAYING REAL

Nobody goes into a new business expecting to fail, but being grown-up enough to recognize the possibility will make it easier to protect what you've already built. In doing that, you not only allow your spouse to sleep better at night, but you'll still have ammo left to wage the battle on 77 another day!

HERBISM: NEVER TELL THE OTHER PLAYER MORE THAN HE HAS TO KNOW ABOUT THE CARDS HE CAN'T SEE.

15
MULTILEVEL MARKETING

(MLM = MAKE LOTS OF MONEY)

Okay, you've read about half of this book and you agree that owning your own business is the key to wealth and happiness, but no matter how hard you try, you can't imagine yourself doing the things necessary to raise the mountain of cash you'll need. You've drawn up your business plan, and the result is an amount that is truly staggering. Should you give up your hopes and dreams and resign yourself to monotony and lottery tickets?

I'm happy to tell you that you have a great alternative, one that costs next to nothing to get involved with and has a proven track record: multilevel marketing (MLM), also known as network marketing. MLM has probably made more people independently wealthy than any other single kind of enterprise.

ENTRY LEVEL

How do you join an MLM network? You are recruited by a current member, who sells you not only on the basis of the product but on "The Plan" or marketing system. This is the program on which, if you stick to it and do it right, you can build your own organization of entrepreneurs. You share your profits with your recruiter, and your recruits share their profits with you, and everybody gets filthy, stinking rich!

Best of all, you can get into MLM with very little money, even the more established ones such as Amway, Shaklee, Tupperware, Herbalife, and NuSkin. These companies sell products that everyone agrees are first-rate — and many fine people are happy to buy.

Well, there must be a downside to all this, right? At least, according to the network news shows, which regularly trot out their MLM abuse stories. And there's no shortage of failures in MLM, just as in any other kind of business. Because it costs little to enter, more people jump into MLM than restaurants or hardware stores or used-car lots. Inevitably some don't get it right. Some try cutting corners. Others shade the truth. People get hurt and start blaming everyone else.

> There's no shortage of failures in MLM, just as in any other kind of business.

DO NOT READ THESE INSTRUCTIONS

Here's a common theme: A distributor invests a ton of cash in inventory and is stuck with it when business fails to materialize. Aha! Fraud, you say. But wait — all the established MLM firms, in the literature they send you, discourage the accumulation of inventory. (And, although I've never been involved in any MLM business, I've read the literature.) So what gives? Well, some fools read the paperwork, toss it aside, and figure they can buy their way into a higher level with the company and their business will catch up later.

80   There are other fools who think they can make a million overnight while sitting on their duffs, and are shocked when they find out it doesn't work that way, and that if they had read the company brochure they would know that.

WHICH SIDE OF THE LAW?

But wait, you say. Aren't all MLMs simply pyramid schemes, in which the early joiners make the most? Yes, of course they are. So are all businesses. There's always someone at the top who's been there a long time, and a few senior people on the next level down, and a whole lot of people just now coming in at the bottom. Is everyone equal at General Electric? Guess again.

In a traditional business, an accomplished employee can leave and use her accumulated skills, experience, earnings, and a few associates to start her own business. Similarly, in a reputable MLM program, the plan is designed so that, upon reaching a certain level of production, the affiliate can break away from the main group with his downline and start his own new organization within the original MLM. That's the magic of it.

In a reputable MLM, the affiliate can break away from the main group and start his own organization within the original MLM.

Of course, some crooks do operate bogus MLMs, and some types of MLMs are illegal. You've got to watch out for these schemes — especially the ones that recruit new members with impossible promises of vast returns. You wouldn't buy a restaurant without checking it out thoroughly, would you? Use your common sense. If it sounds too good to be true, it probably is.

But if you want to be your own boss, starting tomorrow morning, with no money and no know-how, then MLM is for you. It's not as free-wheeling as a traditional business. There's a well-defined track to run on and not much room for new ideas. But these limits help make up for your experience deficit and can give you a feeling of security. In this respect, MLM is 81 a lot like franchising.

IT'S A LIFESTYLE THING

People get into MLM for the lifestyle as much as the money. A few years back I had an Amway distributor named Sonny on my TV show. Sonny had been a fast-food franchisee, and a pretty successful one, but he gave up a lucrative business to get into Amway. Why? I asked him. Because, he said, not only did he make more money with Amway, he now spent most of his time with his family. In the restaurant business, you spend most of your time in the restaurant.

Another MLM friend of mine, Dean, is with Shaklee. Dean is the antithesis of "slick": he's a down-to-earth Midwesterner of few words and more than seventy years. He and his late parents spent thirty years building a multistate organization that now affords Dean an easy life. How does he do it? He lives and breathes Shaklee. He uses and believes in the products. He wears his Shaklee name tag constantly. He hands out literature, tapes, and products to everyone he meets.

To be a success in MLM, you have to love it and to live it. On vacation with my family in Hawaii recently, I was lying by the pool reading a book when a succession of strangers — Diamond Direct Distributors attending an Amway convention in the hotel — came up and asked if I was happy with my career and my life and would I like to change it. I said, "Thanks, but I love what I'm doing. That's my wife and kids over there in the pool, and I've got so much money and happiness I'm writing a book about it!" That barely slowed them down. Talk about overcoming rejection!

There's no mystery why these people are at the top of the MLM business: they know what they're doing, and they believe in it. Most important of all, they share it with everyone. The organization is like a giant support group, and outsiders are potential insiders to be recruited.

MLM people don't have to be slick salespeople. They just need to believe in themselves and their program, live the MLM

82 lifestyle, and be doggedly determined — even in the face of inevitable rejection by strangers and ridicule from friends and enemies alike.

Besides avoiding the fly-by-night operations, what mistakes should you watch out for?

- First, pick just one MLM company and stick with it. Getting involved in more will dilute your effectiveness and seal your doom.

- Second, don't suffer your bad days in silence. Talk with your sponsor and stay motivated.

- Third, remember that MLM is a business that throws you many of the same challenges as any other enterprise.

- Finally, if you're married, try to get your spouse enthusiastically on board. It's a rough road for a lone ranger.

HERBISM: MULTILEVEL MARKETING IS THE EASIEST WAY TO START A NEW BUSINESS — BUT THAT DOESN'T MEAN IT'S EASY.

16
THE FRANCHISING GAME

(BUYING SOMEONE ELSE'S DREAM)

Here's one more alternative to writing your own business plan and finding a rich guy to fund it: franchising. More than a few people have grown filthy, stinking rich by franchising from a regional or national chain. But a franchise is only as good as its parent company, and the quality of the franchise is of the utmost importance.

THE HOLY FORMULA

As the owner of a franchise, you're a lot like the captain of a ship in the navy. You're expected to use your initiative in making the day-to-day operating decisions and take care of challenges and emergencies as they crop up. But you're under strict orders to follow regulations at all times, and woe unto your aspirations if you don't.

84   This rigidity is the product of a hard-fought success story. You're buying a license to use a proven formula, you're backed by enormous resources, and you're practically assured of success. The decisions you're allowed to make are limited in number and scope, which cuts down on your worries, especially if you don't like making decisions. But for satisfactory results, you've got to follow the directions on the box to the letter. Anything less, and all bets are off — and so's the deal.

Want to run a McDonald's? It's not as simple as just buying the building. Every move you make must be exactly as specified by McDonald's headquarters. The folks there have done this hundreds and hundreds of times, so they know what they're doing. They pick the location. They do the traffic counts. They determine the real estate purchase price and negotiate the contracts and leases. They tell you what equipment to buy and who to buy it from. There is zero deviation from one franchise to the next. The people who run McDonald's are absolutely inflexible about quality control — and who can blame them? Their rigidity has served them very well.

> Buying into a quality franchise is as close to a guaranteed success as you can get.

Freedom from tough decisions attracts a lot of people to franchising. They like being told what to do. It provides security. It cuts the risk of making a bad decision. It's made a lot of people a lot of money, and who can argue with that? Buying into a quality franchise operation is as close to a guaranteed success as you can get.

THE COMPANY GIVETH . . .

Another big plus for franchise owners is the public relations support they get from the parent company — primarily the benefit of the company's national marketing program. If you've got a Burger King, you get name recognition from anybody who's ever switched on a TV. The kids holler for Whoppers when Mom or Dad doesn't feel like cooking dinner.

Your name pops into office workers' heads when lunchtime rolls around. Vacationers rolling through town spot your sign three miles away, on that prime Interstate lot your corporation bought for you.

As a franchise owner, you also get a wide range of material, service, and system support, depending on the type of business. The corporation may provide dealer information kits, business cards, brochures, billboard ads, banners, newspaper and Yellow Pages ads, company vehicles, toll-free phone lines, employee training programs, order and inventory forms, and accounting services. You and your employees may be offered medical insurance and retirement programs, free or discounted vacation packages, and the opportunity to attend company conferences in exotic locations.

...AND THE COMPANY TAKETH AWAY

The mother ship does not give you all this support out of the goodness of her heart. First of all, the initial investment is substantial. Where joining a multilevel marketing enterprise costs in the hundreds, getting a good franchise can cost anywhere from tens of thousands to millions of dollars, especially the really great ones that are already established. Our friend Ronald wants to see a million, cash. And you have to tithe: the company skims a percentage off the top.

As a franchise owner, you'll probably find yourself sweating tight budgets, high turnover, long hours, and the aggravations of a high-volume, low-margin business. But, hey, you're running your own business. Sort of.

A SURE THING, FOR A PRICE

Remember what I told you earlier? That to become filthy, stinking rich, you have to take risks? Well, to be perfectly frank about it, franchising doesn't really fit into the model I'm outlining in this book. The risk factor in franchising is smaller than in most small businesses, because the bulk of

86 the risk is assumed by the parent organization. If the folks up at headquarters keep making good decisions, and if you don't doze off and set the place on fire, you'll make more than enough money to take the family out to eat regularly. (To a good restaurant, not that fast-food box you run.)

> To buy into the best franchises, you have to be wealthy to begin with.

On the other hand, to buy into the best franchises, you have to be wealthy to begin with. The big burger boys won't even talk to you seriously unless you have a liquid net worth of at least a million dollars. Anything less, and you're buying into less of a sure thing and more of a risk. And you'd still enjoy few of the freedoms you'd have if you took all the risks yourself and started your own business on your own terms.

That said, there are lots of "up and comers" you can look into. Check out the myriad of books in print on the subject of franchises, visit local business expos, and, of course, browse the Net.

One more thing: just as in starting any business, it's wise to get advice from the professionals. Hire a good lawyer and a good CPA, both experienced with franchise businesses, to check out the paperwork the company sends you. You don't want to find out too late that you've given up necessary legal protections or committed yourself to unfavorable financial terms.

HERBISM: ALL BUSINESSES INVOLVE TRADE-OFFS. FRANCHISES TRADE FREEDOM FOR SECURITY. CAN YOU LIVE WITH THAT?

17
NET
PROFITS

(DOING BUSINESS ONLINE)

magine you're a brilliant scientist, charged by the government with safeguarding its increasingly computerized operations against nuclear attack. How pleasant. Well, your common sense tells you that the more centralized these operations are, the more vulnerable they will be. If you could disperse central control, or even better, eliminate it entirely, then theoretically it would be next to impossible to knock out the system.

Well, that's exactly what our scientists dreamed up not too long ago, and the result is what we now know as the Internet. And if you have any foresight at all, you realize that this one development is without a doubt going to change life on this planet more than any other single invention in human history. It will be the driving force of the global economy in the new century. There's no escaping it.

88   Today, as I write this, economists are divided into two groups, those who get it and those who don't. You see, if you went to business school in any year before, say, 1990, you are totally unprepared for what the Net is going to mean. This is actually pretty cool to me, since in this unique case my total lack of formal higher education is actually a boon. I am unencumbered by what my professors taught me about business. I have no idea what isn't possible, so I feel totally free to make some predictions and to translate it into what it could all mean to you.

MAIN STREET, USA

Let's start with a simple image in your mind. Close your eyes and imagine a beautiful, tree-lined street downtown in Anytown, USA. Neatly parked cars line both sides of the street; smiling pedestrians stroll along browsing in store windows. There's an old-fashioned barbershop with a striped pole, a friendly neighborhood grocer, a haberdasher, and a soda fountain. A jolly Irish policeman strides proudly down the way, wishing all the locals a good day; he plucks a juicy red apple from the grocer's storefront as the proprietor beams approvingly.

There, just down the block, is your store. It's beautiful, successful — your pride and joy. Now just imagine that the camera filming this idyllic scene pans back, giving a nice long-distance frame of the whole peaceful vision.

Hold that thought.

Now imagine the entire thing blowing up right before your very eyes, sending bricks, glass, and debris flying in every direction — because, baby, that's what the Net is going to do to Main Street!

YEAR ZERO OF THE NEW ECONOMY

In the twenty-first century, the Internet will be the very foundation on which the global economy is built. This book is neither science fiction nor futurism, but you can be sure that the entire economic rule book as we have known it is going right out the window. Since there is, by design, no central control of the Net, it is fundamentally impossible to regulate —

so governments will become more and more irrelevant in countries that fully participate in the new global Internet economy. And that certainly includes yours and mine.

What this means to you is simple. I painted that little picture of your store blowing up for another reason. You see, unlike a traditional business whose potential is limited by location, square footage, staff, inventory, and other physical factors, Internet enterprises have no walls and are therefore unlimited in potential. It is this fact that throws so many on Wall Street into confusion. They wonder how stock prices for Internet companies can be so high. Traditional companies eventually slack off after their initial profit growth. This is not so on the Net. After all, Net companies have none of the traditional barriers to growth, like physical location or limited customer base. The world is their oyster!

> Since there is no central control of the Net, it is fundamentally impossible to regulate, so governments will become more and more irrelevant.

Therefore, in choosing your new business idea, if you are so inclined, the Net might be the best place to start. Even if a traditional enterprise is your choice, using the Net to market, sell, distribute, gain information, and do other things can only be to your advantage.

IT'S NOT A DONE DEAL

You know all those dot-com zillionaires you've been reading about? You could be one of them. Happily, for all the euphoria and sizzle, starting a Net company is not fundamentally different from opening a corner store. You're simply dealing with computers and data instead of bricks and mortar. You still need a sound business concept and a rock-solid plan. Therefore, all of the principles outlined in this book still apply. If you ignore them, you *will* fail.

An example of one area of Net business that's ripe for failure is the business of retailing exclusively on the Net. It works great

90 if you have a unique product, such as Land's End's clothes, but it's another thing altogether if your product is not unique to you and your only edge is price.

Think of it this way. Shopping for lots of folks is more than a price experience; it is a pleasure. Therefore, a bricks-and-mortar store like Borders Books can charge a little more in return for the coffee, comfy chairs, and atmosphere. Amazon.com, fatbrain.com, and other online bookstores can offer only low price and a huge selection of titles. So far, at least, Amazon has not turned a profit and, as of this writing, has no announced plan or strategy to do so. We'll have to wait and see.

Lacking the physical amenities in-person shops can provide, the online emporium of the future will have to provide more than just price and selection. It will have to sell intangibles — speed (one-click buying), convenience (no hunting for parking, no standing in line), and extras (online reviews, similar publications, links to related materials). Customer service, as always, is paramount, and the online retailer must sell these unique online customer service advantages. But even with all of this, unless a Net enterprise can charge enough for its product or service to make a profit, it *will* fail. Don't buy into that "new paradigm" horse pucky. Profit is still king!

For you, dear reader, just take this as a caveat emptor. The Internet is new, exciting, and unlimited. But it's not like shooting fish in a barrel. It will take careful planning and thought to succeed, just as in any other business forum ever invented, from the corner store to the shopping mall.

HERBISM: THE INTERNET IS LIKE A STORE WITH NO WALLS WHOSE CUSTOMERS ARE THE ENTIRE POPULATION OF THE PLANET.

18
YOUR PAL, THE "B" WORD

(THE ENTREPRENEUR'S SAFETY NET)

Now that I've got you excited about taking big risks and earning big rewards and making yourself filthy, stinking rich, it seems only appropriate to talk about the downside — the possibility that it won't work out.

Now, I'm going to do the best I can to teach you how to be a big success, but at the same time, when you get out there in the world, you're going to run into things that I cannot possibly predict. If you don't handle those things in the most effective way, you may meet the downside. And the downside here is that you lose. I have lost, more than once. It's important to embrace the fact that failure is a very real possibility.

But the fact that I was able to start all over again and ultimately become filthy, stinking rich I owe to the wonder of bankruptcy. Without bankruptcy laws to protect me, I would

92 still be digging myself out of the hole I dug myself into at twenty-one, just like thousands of other entrepreneurs. Without bankruptcy laws, nobody would be in business. Nobody.

A HAVEN FOR SMALL BUSINESSES

Bankruptcy laws are vital, and you have to be aware of what they are, because you may have to take advantage of them. So here's what they basically say: If your business fails, you can declare yourself insolvent, discharge all of your debts (with the exception of the Internal Revenue Service), and start over again. Now, it does remain on your credit report for ten years, so it's going to be a definite black flag to deal with.

Yes, ten years. Hey — nobody said it was easy! But it is a reasonable stigma and a reasonable price to pay. And after all, let's face it: you messed up. This isn't preschool. We're not playing make-believe with pretend money. You're a grown-up, and you have to take responsibility for your mistakes. But the key thing to remember here is that these laws allow you to start over.

You see, what makes the economy run isn't big business, it's small business. Small business employs many, many, many times the number of people that big business does. Nine out of ten people in the United States don't work for IBM; they work at Joe's Corner Store. What do you think allowed Joe to open his store in the first place? Joe really didn't know much about the bankruptcy laws, but he knew that if his store didn't work, it wasn't the end of the world. If the only possible consequence of Joe's store failing had been Joe wasting away for eternity in a dirty cell in a debtor's prison, Joe would never have opened the store in the first place.

What kind of idiot would take a wild risk with everything he owned if failure meant he would probably end up in jail?

The American economy loves small businesses and is custom-tailored to help you in times of failure. Bankruptcy laws protect entrepreneurs. No one would ever start any business if these laws didn't exist. Think about it. What kind of idiot would take a wild risk with everything he owned if failure meant he would probably end up in jail? There's a big difference between taking an intelligent risk and doing something completely senseless. In America, starting your own business is an intelligent risk.

NO SHAME IN RISK

Now there are some people out there who think that bankruptcy laws are some form of cheating. That's nonsense. It's easy for the guy who inherited the company from Daddy to be pissed off when somebody he sold something to goes bankrupt and doesn't have to pay what he or she owes him. But what that spoiled brat doesn't realize is that Daddy would never have started that business had it not been for the safety net of bankruptcy laws.

One more thing. If people give you a hard time and look down their nose at you because you went bankrupt, ignore them. They are people who never took a chance themselves. They're jealous. Other businesspeople — people who have tried and failed and tried and failed — will admire you for taking the chance. Among entrepreneurs, it's almost a badge of honor. If you go broke, you go broke. Pick yourself up, dust yourself off, and try again.

HERBISM: REPEAT AFTER ME: BANKRUPTCY LAW IS OUR FRIEND.

PART III

MAKE IT WORK

(Growing Your Dough)

19
YOUR
GANG

(RUB-A-DUB-DUB, THREE MEN IN A TUB)

Okay, you've got your money in place and you're ready to grab the brass ring. There's a few things you still need. It's a tough world out there, and you need protection. You need allies. Come closer. I want you to meet your three new best friends: your banker, your accountant, and your (shudder!) lawyer.

You think I'm exaggerating? I'm not. You'll need all three of these dudes (or dudettes) solidly in your corner before you bounce into the ring and start bobbing and weaving, jabbing and feinting with your opponents.

YOUR BANKER

The banker and the entrepreneur have an odd relationship, because they are fundamentally different creatures. Entrepreneurs take aggressive risks. Bankers are the most risk-wary people in the world. They aren't impressed by flash; they're scared by it. An entrepreneur hears the words "aggressive business strategy" and thinks "great business opportunity." A banker thinks "chaos and death." The best you can hope for? A banker who hears "aggressive business strategy" and thinks "Hm. Let's at least take a look at the risk and see what the opportunity is." That's bodaciously adventurous for your average banker.

There are two kinds of banks to avoid: consumer banks (banks that cater to regular folks with checkbooks) and big national banks. Big national banks tend to have miles of red tape — forms, applications, committees — and are less likely to approve a first-time entrepreneur who doesn't have much experience or collateral. Consumer banks are not likely to have the financial resources or capabilities to support a business.

Generally, smaller business banks are the best way to go. When you approach a bank, find out first what percentage of its lending is with small businesses like yours. Try to meet with the top executive at the local level. Ask questions to see whether this is the right bank for your business:

1. "When I say the word 'risk,' what's the first thing that comes to your mind?" If the answer is anything that reflects terror or pain, the interview is over.

2. "What kind of services would you provide for me as a small, new entrepreneur?"

3. "How can you help me grow?"

4. "What other small businesses do you support?"

5. "Can I have a list of these clients to contact?"

YOUR ACCOUNTANT

No business owner is ever happy to see the IRS on the doorstep announcing a random audit, but this scenario is an ugly reality of business. Your accountant will quickly become your hero when an auditor comes a-knockin'. You see, the IRS and Congress create or change about a gajillion tax laws every year — far too many for the average untrained schmoe (like me) to keep up with. Without an accountant to pilot you through, it's easy to trip over the red tape of Tax Land.

So how do you find this superhero in disguise? Simple. Ask around. There's no surer sign of a good accountant than happy customers. Ask other professionals which accountants they use — in particular, accountants who specialize in your size or type of business. Pretty soon, regardless of the size of your community, you'll begin to hear the same names again and again. Make a list, and call each of their offices to set up an interview.

> **Without an accountant to pilot you through, it's easy to trip over the red tape of Tax Land.**

Yes, an interview! This is an important decision. Don't base yours on who has the prettiest ad in the Yellow Pages. Find out what the person is like. Don't be afraid to ask questions. Here are a few:

1. "How aggressive are you with the IRS?"

2. "How often are we going to see each other?"

3. "What are you going to charge me?"

4. "Who are your existing customers?"

5. "Can I have a list of referrals?"

One final tip: Always go with a CPA, rather than a tax preparer or a bookkeeper. This is the one instance where education and credentials are everything.

YOUR LAWYER

When you start your business, you'll need a good lawyer to prepare the necessary forms and documents for whatever business structure you choose. Your attorney can also provide invaluable advice on how to prevent trouble down the road, like preparing solid contracts for employees. We live in a society where every perceived slight can be grounds for litigation. To become a successful entrepreneur, you have to be out there and aggressive, always doing something to improve your business. Inevitably you're going to step on somebody's toes, and the person attached to them will respond by taking a whack at you in court.

Most lawsuits are unjustified — especially yours. But there's no use climbing up on a soapbox and shouting about how right you are and how wrong the person suing you is. The civil justice system of the United States cares little about who's right and who's wrong — just who has the best lawyer. You may be the sweetest, most honest, most inoffensive person on the planet, but as an entrepreneur you will at some point be threatened with a lawsuit. Get yourself one hell of a lawyer.

The true gauge of a good lawyer is not how many cases she's won, but how many cases she's settled before they get to court.

The true gauge of a good lawyer is not how many cases she's won, but how many she's settled, to the satisfaction of her clients, before they get to court. Lawsuits are very time-consuming, and time is the most precious of all your resources. When presented with a lawsuit you feel is unjustified, you must ask yourself whether it's worth your time to litigate. If an ex-employee files a wrongful dismissal suit for $5,000 and you know damn well that there was nothing wrongful about the way you handled his dismissal, you need to evaluate the situation. Sit down with your lawyer and discuss it. If a trial is going to cost you $7,000 in legal fees and a week's worth of your time, is it really worth it just to prove that you're right? I don't think so. Don't waste your time. Pay the employee and move on.

So how do you find this Wonder Lawyer? Just as with the 101 accountant, ask around. Find a lawyer who specializes in your kind of business. Approach fellow businesspeople. Ask any lawyers you know, if they were getting sued, who would they choose to represent them? If they choose themselves, forget 'em. Once you've developed a list of potentials, line up the interviews. There are only two questions you need to ask a prospective attorney:

1. "Confronted with the business situation of a lawsuit, would you rather litigate or settle?" If the answer is "When the cost of litigation is more than what could be won, I prefer to settle," you ask,

2. "When can you start?"

If she starts using phrases like "proving your point" or "I'd like to take on that smug bastard," forget her.

KEEPING FRIENDS CLOSE

The best advice I can offer in reference to all three of your new best friends? Be thorough in your research. Take plenty of time to make your decision. Establish good relationships at the very beginning, and stick with the same people for as long as possible.

HERBISM: ASK AROUND. INTERVIEW. CHOOSE WISELY. PAY WELL.

20
YOUR
STREETCORNER

(PUT YOUR BUSINESS IN THE RIGHT PLACE)

The other day, I drove by the absolute dumbest thing that I have ever seen: a freestanding teddy bear store. Boy oh boy — is that store doomed! Maybe, just maybe, it could make it if it were a

big, beautiful building with a huge window displaying hundreds of cute teddy bears in a place with lots and lots of foot traffic constantly moving by it. But in a small, freestanding building segregated from any other structure, without any attractive window display or sign, on a busy urban street devoid of parking that you never pull off of unless you absolutely have to — that store's days are numbered. I promise you. It doesn't matter what's inside. They could be giving away gold-plated teddy bears; no one's ever going to know it.

That cursed store illustrates a very important but often 103 overlooked aspect of business: location. You could start the perfect business and do everything exactly right, but if you don't put your business in the right place, none of it matters. Location is vital. The right place to locate your business depends on three main factors: the type of business you own, your clientele, and the demographics of the area you live in.

TO SEE, OR NOT TO SEE

If you are in retail sales or offer any kind of service that requires the customer to come to you, you must put your business in an easily accessible spot. Your potential customers should not have to beat a path to your door; you should beat the path for them. Your business should be in a high-traffic area with hordes of shoppers walking by every day. If you're in a strip mall, make sure there's a strong anchor tenant that will draw traffic past your shop. Ample parking is a must, as is a clearly visible façade. Remember, the business you're opening is probably going to face

Make your business easy to see and easy to get to.

same-city competition. Don't give your potential customer any reason to go to your competition instead of coming to you. Make your business easy to see and easy to get to.

Conversely, if you own a business that customers are never going to set foot in, your main concern is to be accessible to what you need. For example, if you're in a business where you're going to be shipping a lot of goods, it's really smart to be out by the airport so that you can save time and resources when transporting your goods. Or if you're starting a computer consulting business where you make house calls to people's homes and offices to fix their computer glitches, your home base should be centrally located. That way you'll have more potential customers within a short drive of your business.

WHO GOES THERE?

The second thing you need to think about when hunting for office space is your clientele. For example, a large percentage of my clients are elderly retirees. Therefore, I cannot be in a building that requires my clients to walk up a flight of stairs. What do you sell? Plumbing supplies? A plumbing store wouldn't do too well deep inside a mega-mall.

Finally, consider the demographics: weather, population, traffic congestion, and other such city-specific issues. Here in Tucson, it hits 105 degrees four months out of the year and a chilling 72 degrees in winter. Malls are enclosed, parking is covered, everything is air-conditioned. No one is going to face the heat of Hades to come to an outdoor café in Tucson, no matter how good the food is. Or take New York City: not a very mobile population. No one's going to schlepp forty-three blocks across town in bumper-to-bumper traffic to get to your bagel joint — regardless of how much you advertise — when there's another bagelry two blocks from home.

There are many other factors to take into account when looking for a business location. My advice? Two main points. Point number one: Identify your targeted customer and go from there. Take her needs into consideration above all else. Point two: You're a customer of a dozen different businesses every day. Why do you shop where you shop and hire the services that you hire? Think like the customer that you are, and decisions will come naturally to you.

HERBISM: DON'T MAKE CUSTOMERS BEAT A PATH TO YOUR DOOR. BEAT THE PATH FOR THEM.

21
YOUR HOME, OR YOUR OFFICE?

(DON'T DECORATE A WAREHOUSE)

f you've decided to start up a service business, one of the nicer realities of today's world is that in many service industries you get to choose between working out of a traditional office or an office in your home. Just like location, this is an important decision. But whichever you choose, the look of your physical space is vital. Choose wrong and your business will soon have a flat EEG.

Years ago, I had a friend who inherited an interior design firm from his father. In its early years the business had been a strong success, but since then its profits had slowly declined. Passing the baton to the son made no difference. The business continued to deteriorate as high-scale corporate clients were gradually replaced by chintzy, low-profile customers. Throughout the life of the business and until its final demise a few years

106 ago, its owner and employees made lots of excuses for why business was slackening: the economy had changed, the city's demographics were shifting, their ad campaign was ill-focused, and so on. But the real reason the business died a long, slow, painful death had nothing to do with any of those excuses, nor was it a reflection of the competency of its principals. The problem was the office building.

You see, in the late 1960s his father had built a then-modern office building, very much in the style of the day, to house the firm. However, when my friend inherited the business in the early 1980s, he picked up right where his father had left off, now-antiquated office building and all. And to the day in the late 1990s when he closed the doors on his firm for the last time, they were still the doors of that old-fashioned, outdated, horribly ugly office building — doors that the Brady Bunch wouldn't have been caught dead opening.

DRESS UP PRESENTATION SPACE

The business of interior design is very much a business of style and modernity. Of course there is the pragmatic side of actually furnishing a home or office, but the aesthetic value is just as important. So answer me this: Would you, the customer, hand over a large chunk of your hard-earned cash for the service and style of a bunch of people working in an office straight out of *The Mod Squad*? Of course you wouldn't.

In business, you must be housed in a manner appropriate to the industry.

The moral of the story is that in business you must be housed in a manner appropriate to the industry. Are you selling your expertise, convenience, or intimate, one-on-one relationships? Then the coziness of a home office might be for you. This would also be true if most of your business were conducted on the road or over the telephone. Does your business depend on the image of success, have a lot of foot traffic, need plenty of conference or meeting space, or require a more professional feel? In that case, a traditional office is best.

Remember, also, that if you are in any kind of business where you're being highly paid for a product or service, whatever your customer sees had better be impressive. If you're going to open an interior design firm, the office building should be brand new and beautiful, the walls should be alive with color, and the décor of the building should be clean and modern. How do you finance all of this? It's included in the business plan as an absolutely mandatory expense.

The bottom line: Your office is like your clothes. Make sure it's tailored to your image and to the expectations of your customers or clients.

DRESS DOWN WORK SPACE

On the opposite end of the spectrum, a few years ago there was a big, multilevel marketing firm here in Tucson that happened to be leasing office space in the same building I was in. They grew and expanded quickly — and went bankrupt just as fast. At one point, this company was occupying four entire floors of an upscale office building — three of which they were using to pack boxes — at the rate of $20 a square foot! Talk about a truly idiotic waste of money. Granted, they were in a business that entailed impressing and recruiting people. But they could have leased one floor for that pur-

You need to look sharp only where the customer is going to see it.

pose, and gotten all the packing space their little hearts desired down by the airport for $4 a square foot.

That company got so drunk with success that they stopped controlling costs. No matter how successful your business becomes and no matter how much money you make, there's never a need to waste it. If all you need is a warehouse to pack boxes, rent a warehouse! There are lots of businesses that the customer is never going to set foot in. As long as these places

108 are clean, safe working environments for your employees, who cares what they look like? You need to look sharp only where the customer is going to see it.

HERBISM: IF YOU'RE OPENING A MAIL ORDER OR INTERNET BUSINESS, YOUR OFFICE DOESN'T HAVE TO BE THE TAJ MAHAL.

22
LOOKIN' GOOD

(LITTLE THINGS MEAN A LOT)

At the risk of sounding superficial, I'm going to be brutally honest with you: Looks matter. A lot. You don't need to be a supermodel strutting down the runway, but you must put a lot of effort into your physical appearance. In all business, but especially in small business, your personal appearance and reputation are of the utmost importance.

There's no denying it, people are naturally drawn to attractive, successful people. Regardless of how fair or sensible that may or may not be, that's the way it is. It's just human nature, so accept it. What this means to you as an aspiring entrepreneur is that even if you're not successful early in your career,

110 you must behave as if you are. You must get yourself into the mind-set of being a success, and the truth will follow.

LOOK THE PART

Specifically, this means dressing the part — whatever part that may be. The particulars are different for every type of business, but the general idea is the same across the board. Stop for a minute and think of successful people you know in any business. Notice the details of their appearance: their clothes hang just right, their hair is in place, they carry themselves well — they're impeccable. When I say "appearance," I don't mean how attractive you are, I mean how well you present yourself.

This is especially crucial to small-business owners. In the beginning, you *are* the business. You'll be doing all the work yourself: gaining the support of investors, initiating and maintaining business relationships, interacting with customers and clients, hiring employees, and so on. Your physical presentation represents how you conduct business. An investment in your appearance is an investment in your business. No detail is too small.

It's the attention to a myriad of details that creates the overall impression of quality.

Take TV, for example. Why do network broadcasts look better than local ones? It's the little things you see without being aware of them: set design, lighting angles, computer graphics, positioning of on-air people, and hundreds of other refinements. Experienced people and generous budgets make a difference, but it's the attention to a myriad of details that creates the overall impression of quality.

If you're starting your own real estate business, you'd best pick up your clients in a nice-sized, comfy-cozy luxury car. Who's going to buy a $300,000 house from a guy in an '83 Subaru? Get a new Cadillac, Lexus, or Mercedes. Keep it shiny and clean. Factor the lease into your business plan so that it's always taken care of.

The same goes for your personal appearance. If you're a consultant starting a new firm — man or woman — you'd better wear high-quality, perfectly tailored suits to the office. And cheap imitations won't cut it. However subtle you may think the discrepancy is, the actual difference between a nice business suit and a discount business suit is startlingly obvious. Don't think for a minute that a J. C. Penny suit is equal in quality to a Brooks Brothers. It's not.

Of course, you must tailor your appearance to your industry. If you're running a construction company, you're going to look like a moron pulling up to the site driving a Cadillac sedan and wearing a business suit. Better: jeans and a casual shirt — high-quality jeans (that fit. No, Bubba, you don't wear the same size you did in high school. Your jeans must button around your waist, not your genitals!), high-quality shirt. And drive a truck or sport-utility vehicle — but a brand spankin' new one. Remember, you're the boss!

BEHAVE YOURSELF

This philosophy also extends to your behavior. If you pull up to a restaurant in a vehicle painted with "Sally's Flower Shop" and you're a jerk to your waitress, word will travel fast that you, Sally, are an unspeakable pain in the ass, and your business will suffer just as surely as the sun will rise tomorrow. Always conduct yourself in public as your business's good-will ambassador. Every action you take — however insignificant you may think it is — reflects upon you as a businessperson. You cannot be a jerk and expect your business to thrive.

> Always conduct yourself in public as your business's good-will ambassador. You cannot be a jerk and expect your business to thrive.

This may seem like a strange thing to include in a business book, but it's perfectly relevant. You cannot cut corners where self-presentation is concerned. People pick up on a thousand little subliminal messages that

112 you communicate through the details of your appearance and behavior. This is not something you can afford to mess up. Tiny pebbles start huge landslides.

HERBISM: YOU'LL NEVER GET RICH LOOKING POOR.

23
YOUR MORAL COMPASS

(WHAT WOULD YOUR KIDS SAY?)

There's one rule that governs every move I make, both at work and in my personal life: I never do anything that I wouldn't be proud to tell my children about. It's a good rule. In order to adhere to it, I follow three guidelines: I always keep my word, I never lie, and I never cut corners.

IT'S GOOD BUSINESS

Keeping your word makes you an honorable individual, and honorable individuals make honorable business-people. By honorable, I mean doing the right thing even when nobody is looking. Regardless of how small the promise

114 or to whom you make it, you must follow through on it; that's the only way to conduct business. A contract should never be necessary except as a technicality. Every business deal should be incumbent upon nothing more than your word and your handshake.

> Every business deal should be incumbent upon nothing more than your word and your handshake.

If keeping your word is policy, then it follows that lying is unacceptable. Intentional deceit is rude and annoying coming from anyone, but an employer lying to his or her employees or clients is absolutely inexcusable. Quite frankly, it's business suicide.

SOCIAL LIES AND COWARDLY LIES

Now, I know we don't live on Planet Honesty. There are certain types of socially permissible lies that everyone tells and everyone accepts. Your secretary comes to work wearing the new earrings her husband gave her for her birthday — and they're atrocious; she asks what you think of them; you tell her they're lovely; she knows you're lying, and she's grateful. Your brother is losing his hair; he asks you nervously how his new hairpiece looks; although you've never seen one at any price that didn't look like a hair hat, of course you tell him he looks great. These are social lies. They aren't so much lies as good manners.

> Social lies aren't so much lies as good manners. They have a kind and justifiable motivation: to spare someone's feelings.

They have a kind and justifiable motivation: to spare someone's feelings. Those aren't the lies I'm talking about.

Here's the kind of lies I'm talking about: Promising an employee a raise you have no intention of delivering. Giving a phony excuse for canceling a meeting. Accepting a deadline you know you can't meet. I don't get it. Why lie? If you can't afford to give your employee a raise, don't string him along by making empty promises. If you canceled a meeting to have lunch with an old friend who's in town, just say so. If a client wants a project delivered by an unrealistic date, simply apologize and explain to her why it's not possible. Just be honest!

> In business, your employees' and clients' trust in you is the only thing that matters.

Habitual liars defend themselves by saying that little lies aren't malicious and that they don't tell lies with the intention of hurting anybody. What they don't seem to realize is that the motivation doesn't matter. Whether you mean to hurt anybody or not, at the very least you hurt yourself because you undermine other people's confidence in you. And in business, your employees' and clients' trust in you is the only thing that matters. A lie is a lie, whatever your definition of the word "is" is. No matter how you dress it up, it's still a violation of trust.

In business you will often be presented with a not-quite-honest shortcut. Don't ever take it. Whether it's blatantly immoral or just slightly into that fuzzy gray area between ethical and unethical, cutting two days off a project or saving 15 percent on a purchase is not worth risking your reputation. Character isn't everything — it's the only thing. Take my advice: Always take the long cut. You'll sleep better at night.

HOW DO YOU WANT TO BE TREATED?

All of this basically boils down to one thing: the Golden Rule. "Do unto others as you would have others do unto you." Yep — it's considered golden for a good reason! If everyone practiced that one simple rule, there really wouldn't be much else to worry about. As a businessman and an employer, I strive to do this every day. I treat my employees and

116 clients with respect and dignity, and that's how I expect to be treated in return. I know these are things we all learn in preschool, but the whole of the business world seems to have forgotten them. Set yourself apart from the mass of society by behaving yourself.

HERBISM: IN BUSINESS, YOU ARE ONLY AS GOOD AS YOUR REPUTATION, AND YOU CAN LOSE YOUR REPUTATION ONLY ONCE. BE CAREFUL.

24
GO TO
MARKET

(GET YOUR NAME BEFORE THE PUBLIC)

No matter how good a mousetrap you build, people will never know about it unless you tell them.

That's what your marketing strategy is all about. It is not a luxury and it is not an optional expense. Marketing is absolutely mandatory. Consider it a top priority, no less important than paying your rent.

THE THREE-LEGGED RACE

Let's start by defining marketing as any action taken to publicize your business and increase its revenue. Marketing is a threefold venture that includes advertising, public relations, and selling — three very different components often confused by entrepreneurs, a confusion that all too

118 frequently leads to unconvincing and inadequate marketing plans. And if you don't have a successful marketing campaign, you don't have a business.

Advertising means paying money to directly publicize your business through some form of media. An ad in the Sunday paper that alerts the public to your clothing store's semiannual clearance sale; a thirty-second spot on the radio announcing the grand opening of your restaurant; a TV commercial depicting a map of the city, spotlighting all three of your car repair shops — these are all examples of advertising.

Public relations is the indirect promotion and publicizing of yourself and your business. You don't buy this kind of attention; you earn it. Donating funds to a local homeless shelter; sponsoring a Little League team in your neighborhood; volunteering your time or providing supplies to any charitable or philanthropic cause — these actions may not directly influence sales, but they get your name out there and generate confidence in you and your business. No amount of paid advertising can do that.

> Charitable actions may not directly influence sales, but they get your name out there and generate confidence in you and your business.

Selling consists of all the actions you perform to elicit a specific response: a sale. Selling is how your receptionist answers the phone, how attractive and tidy you keep your store or office, how you treat a customer or client in your office or store, how you treat her after she leaves, and especially how you close the deal.

The object of public relations is to get your name out there and raise awareness of your business. You want to make your name synonymous with the industry you work in, so that when potential customers have a need for your type of product or service, they immediately think of you. The object of advertising is to get the customer to your place of business right then and there. The object of selling is to get the customer to hand over the cash! Individually, each action has its own specific goals. But only when all three are addressed appropriately can a marketing plan be truly successful.

The thing to remember here is that regardless of any other considerations, you must take action on your marketing plan so your customers can find you. How do I do this? you ask. An advertising agency? Yes and no. Ad agencies, marketing experts, and public relations firms can be invaluable if — and this is a big if — they are legitimate. Be careful; any schmoe can hang a sign on his door and call himself an advertising consultant. Unlike the lawyers or CPAs you will meet when starting your own business, marketers and advertisers don't have to go to school or get a license.

So how can you tell the good from the bad from the ugly? Ask around. There's no better proof of a competent marketing firm than happy clients. Ask friends and fellow businesspeople which firms they use and recommend. Then call up the firms, tell them you're interested in hiring them, and ask for a list of their clients that you can contact. Any reputable firm will gladly offer you a list of referrals, as they shouldn't have anything to hide.

THE BIG TWO

Now for your two biggest concerns: time and money. How much of each should you expect to commit to marketing? Quite a bit. The first six months of business will be the most intense; you'll really have to fight to make your name recognizable. During these crucial introductory months, you should double your standard monthly marketing budget. For example, if you're planning to devote 12 percent of your overall budget to marketing long-term, double that to 24 percent for the first six months. It may sound like a sizable chunk, but

> If you don't market yourself well, you might as well not market yourself at all.

if you don't market yourself well, you might as well not market yourself at all. As a general guideline, service businesses should allocate no less than 10 percent of their budget to marketing; retail, no less than 15 percent.

120   As far as time is concerned, there's no such thing as too much marketing and — except for criminal behavior — no such thing as bad publicity. Seize any and every opportunity to promote your business. If sales are higher than you planned and revenue is up, reinvest that unexpected cash right back into the business with more marketing. Business isn't going well? Reallocate your funds and sink as much money as you can into advertising. Repetition, repetition, repetition. It's the only way.

HERBISM: BEAT THE HORSE UNTIL IT'S DEAD — THEN BEAT IT SOME MORE.

25

CUSTOMERS
WHO COME BACK

(DON'T DROP THE MATCH IN YOUR OWN DYNAMITE)

There are two things you can do that will sink your business faster than the *Titanic*: make false promises to your customers, and over-sell. The first is an unacceptable act of deceit. The second is an honest mistake that comes from inexperience.

ANGRY CUSTOMERS TALK MORE

False promises and bogus guarantees are the blood-suckers attached to otherwise ethical businesses. A person can own and operate a legitimate business, pay his taxes, treat his employees fairly, and be an all-around good person, but if he hands his customers phony guarantees, none of it matters. His business will inevitably go under.

122 If you own a retail shop that backs up its sales with false promises or a no-refund policy, I've got news for you: You've got yourself a dandy going-out-of-business policy. When it comes to customer satisfaction, word of mouth is the strongest, swiftest form of communication. Nothing angers customers more than feeling cheated or betrayed, and angry customers are the most talkative. Don't raise clients' expectations if you have no intention of delivering. In any business — retail or service — implement fair policies on returns, exchanges, and refunds for dissatisfied customers; keep them clearly posted where the customer can see them; and always honor them. If you underpromise and overdeliver, you'll never have a problem.

> **When it comes to customer satisfaction, word of mouth is the strongest, swiftest form of communication.**

SELL IT AND SHUT UP

The second-biggest no-no in business is the oversell. You've spent a fortune on advertising, you've marketed your high-quality product or service, the customer is through the front door, she's heard and absorbed your sales pitch, she's reaching for her credit card — and you just can't shut up. You continue to sing the praises of your product or service, you bad-mouth your competition, you compliment the customer on what a smart choice she's made, and on and on and on!

How many times have you been the customer in that situation? Plenty of times, I'm sure. And what's your reaction? "Boy, I'm never coming here again!" It leaves a bitter taste in your mouth. Overselling is the worst kind of selling because it squashes any chance of repeat business.

Every person has her own built-in sales tolerance. How do you know when she's reached that limit? Simple. She either says no thanks and leaves, or she says yes and reaches for her money. At that point, there are only two sentences you should 123 utter: "Thank you very much" and "I hope to see you again." Then shut up and smile.

HERBISM: REPEAT BUSINESS IS THE BEST KIND OF BUSINESS. DON'T DO ANYTHING TO DISSUADE YOUR CUSTOMERS FROM COMING BACK FOR SECONDS.

26
RESPECT YOUR COMPETITION

(WALK SOFTLY AROUND A SLEEPING GORILLA)

The thrill of starting your very own business — dreaming up a great idea, attracting investors, quitting your job — can give you a heck of a rush. It can inspire you to take on the competition in full force. Good for you. Just be careful not to wake a sleeping gorilla.

No matter what industry you're in, other companies have beat you to it. Most have been only moderately successful, but every industry has its giant. My advice to you? Don't make beating this competitor at all costs your life's mission. Irritating a major corporation or a big, successful store is not the way to fame and fortune. They may be sitting across the street from your shop, quietly going about their business of raking in millions of dollars a day, seemingly oblivious to the existence of your business. But trust me, if you so much as do one thing that angers a major force in the industry, they'll squash you like a bug. They have the resources, the manpower, and the experience to do it without a moment's hesitation.

THE ARIZONA CHICKEN WAR

Fifteen years ago in Tucson there was a great place called Pollo Asado that served grilled chicken. Tasty, said Pollo Asado's ads. A lot better for you than that greasy fried stuff. Pollo Asado was a local success story.

Then Pollo Asado did something stupid. In an aggressive advertising push, the grilled-chicken upstart took a slap at the sleeping gorilla. Its new TV ads featured a white-haired Southern gentleman — complete with goatee, white suit, and string tie — keeling over from a heart attack. From eating greasy fried chicken, of course.

It wasn't long before KFC introduced its own line of roasted chicken and sprinkled a few of its megadollars into a national ad campaign that attracted Pollo Asado's health-conscious customers. Pollo Asado never recovered.

In other words, play nice. No mud-slinging. No name-calling. No bad-mouthing. Play nice with the other kids, especially the kids that are bigger than you. These are the unwritten rules of business. You can be aggressive without being foolish.

HERBISM: DON'T PISS OFF THE BIG BOYS.

27
HEY! YOU'RE THE BOSS!

(BECOMING AN EMPLOYER)

Wow! You're starting your own business! You conceived the business idea. You quit your old job. You bought the business planning software.

You picked your banker, your accountant, and your lawyer.

You named your business. You wrote the proposal. You raised the capital. You arranged the marketing. You selected the location. You even designed the cute little logo on your business cards, brochures, and signs.

Now you've opened your doors for business, a few months have passed, and you've made it through the opening crunch. Your idea works, and you're making money. But you're working harder than when you were back in that little cubicle. You really need to take time off and relax, but you can't afford to close up and go away.

From one entrepreneur to another, I have some good news and some bad news for you. The good news: It's time for you to become the boss! You need to hire an employee or two — to begin assembling the winning team, the talented troupe that's going to carry you to Filthy Stinking Rich Land.

Sounds easy, doesn't it? You'd be surprised. And that's the bad news: This new business is your baby, and it's hard to let go. But just like any child, if you smother it with too much attention, you'll spoil it.

YOU ARE NOT INDISPENSABLE

Let me come right out and say it: You cannot do it all. I know you think you can, but you can't. No one can. You have to learn to trust your business to the competent hands of employees — perhaps the hardest thing for any entrepreneur to do. After all, you've invested a lot of yourself in this business! But it's impossible to become truly successful without learning to depend on other people. You must delegate responsibility. If you can't learn to loosen your grip, you're going to end up being a stressed-out, uptight, egomaniacal control freak. What's the point of being self-employed if you don't reap the lifestyle benefits it offers?

> **You have to learn to trust your business to the competent hands of your employees — perhaps the hardest thing for any entrepreneur to do.**

I know, I know — it's tough to share control of the business, even though you know it's necessary. Entrepreneurs know they cannot retain complete control over every aspect of the business, so they hire employees — as if they could actually let them do their work! I've seen it a hundred times. Once they've hired the employees, they constantly look over their shoulders and check up on them every twenty seconds. The entrepreneur thinks that he's helping, but really all he's doing is being a jerk.

PULL, DON'T PUSH

Now that you are the head honcho, sit back and enjoy the benefits. Let your employees help and support you. Your job is to be a leader, not a dictator. Some people think that since they pay their people, they own them. This is not feudal England. This is not the Old South. You cannot have slaves, serfs, or indentured servants. You have employees and co-workers — and if you treat them with respect, they will follow you willingly. Second-guessing your employees' every move will only devalue and insult them — and devalued, insulted employees don't stick around for long.

Look, gang, this is one of the coolest things about being self-employed. Not only are you your own boss, you're *the* boss! Just remember always what it was like before you hit it big, and you'll have the whole employer-employee thing nailed!

HERBISM: YOU HIRED THEM. YOU TRAINED THEM. YOU TRUSTED THEM WITH THE JOB. NOW SHUT UP AND LET THEM DO IT!

28
FIND THE HIDDEN TALENT

(LOOK PAST THE RÉSUMÉ)

No one is born without talent. In fact, most people have a million little talents hidden away, out of sight — talents that don't necessarily show up on a résumé. As an employer, your job is to discover your employees' hidden talents. More accurately, you must give your employees the freedom to discover their own hidden talents.

IN TWENTY-FIVE WORDS OR LESS . . .

About résumés. Let's see: A person is supposed to document her education, summarize her entire professional background, and express her personality on one side of an eleven-inch sheet of paper? Give me a break! A résumé is as far as you can get from accurately representing a person.

130   The only purpose of the résumé is to express an individual's interest in filling a position at your company, and for that it's a useful tool. But when a hirer uses a résumé as a basis for passing final judgment, he's given that flimsy piece of paper far more weight than it deserves. Unless the résumé cites a screamingly obvious problem — involvement in the KKK, changing jobs every thirty days — you cannot eliminate a job candidate without ever having met or talked with him, any more than you should hire him solely on the basis of words on paper.

When you advertise a position to be filled, you're likely to get dozens, even hundreds, of applicants. Make it easy on yourself: screen out the obvious misfits by using the telephone. Invite the rest in for an interview. You'll learn a lot that the résumé didn't tell you: how well the candidate relates to others face-to-face; his ability to think on his feet, solve problems, and formulate answers; dress, grooming, and posture (especially important for sales positions); general health and physical condition; and, if you're an intuitive person, certain intangibles you can't quite put into words.

SCHOOL IS NOT A RULE

Employers tend to overrate the importance of a potential employee's educational background. I believe in higher education. I think it's a wonderful thing, and I heartily encourage it for all four of my children. But in twenty-plus years of hiring employees, I have found that personal quality, level of adjustment, and happiness in life have no relation whatsoever to which educational institution someone went to and what her grade point average was. If she graduated from college and went on to get a postgraduate degree — good for her! But it's really low on my totem pole of qualifications. I've never seen hard proof of the much-vaunted excellent school–excellent employee correlation.

> In a small office, personalities come first, education and experience a distant second.

There's one thing, and one thing only, that I look for in a job 131 candidate: a personality that meshes with mine. If you work in a small office, regardless of what kind of business you're in, the personalities of the people working in such close quarters come first; education and experience run a distant second. I'm an over-the-top crazy, and I look for someone who can laugh. A little chuckle goes a long way with me. Give me a likable, inexperienced person who's fun to be with and eager to learn over an educated, super-experienced stick-in-the-mud any day!

STOP, LOOSEN UP, AND LISTEN

Once you've hired an employee, climb down off your pedestal! This is an essential part of being a successful employer, but most entrepreneurs are incapable of doing it. They get caught up in the hierarchy of the business food chain. Instead of loosening up and getting to know their employees, they focus on "I'm the boss. You're the employee." Trust me, you'll never succeed with that attitude.

Great people — I guarantee you — have gone unnoticed in every field because their supervisors were unable to get past their own big-boss mentality. When you look at great writers or great actors or great anythings, there are a million people out there who are just as good. The only difference is that the successful people were spotted by someone who took time to spot their potential and develop it. It's true in every field.

> Great people have gone unnoticed in every field because their supervisors were unable to get past their own big-boss mentality.

Tom Clancy was an insurance agent before he became a best-selling novelist. Scott Adams, the creator of the "Dilbert" comic strip, was lost in the chain of command at a communications corporation. It's true, given their creativity, that these worthies would probably have ended up working for themselves anyway, but think how valuable their talent would have been to the company had their employer discovered and used it!

132   I have an employee named Victoria who, over the years, has come to be my most trusted associate. But if I had stubbornly insisted on her doing the job I first wanted her to do, I would have fired her years ago. I hired her to be my assistant, which requires close attention to detail and the ability to cogently put together a sentence. It became startlingly obvious after a very short while that she was all wrong for the position.

At the time, I was expanding my business into media and public speaking. I needed someone to delegate to. So here's what I did. I stepped back and gave Victoria a little room. And, voilà! As it turns out, Victoria's talents are artistic and creative, even though I hired her to be administrative. Rarely do you get the perfect employee in the perfect position on the first shot.

I hired Victoria for the best reason there is: I liked her. She ended up coordinating my television show, designing my promotional ads, arranging my speaking engagements, and being invaluable to me in more ways than I can count. She even passed the very tough Series 7 Securities Exam to become a licensed stockbroker, developed her own clientele, and became a strong revenue source for our firm. Vic has grown to be the most loyal of all my employees by far — she'd be loyal to me even if it cost her — and loyalty is something I've learned to value above all else.

RECIPROCATE LOYALTY

Working with someone will let you discover her hidden talents, but you'll never get that far if you chuck her aside at the first mistake. Before you fire someone because she's not working out exactly the way you thought she would in the position you hired her for, try changing the job description to suit her talents. Every business has different tasks; give your trusted employee a shot at all of them before giving up the ship.

In the big picture, loyalty is the most important part of any business relationship. If an employee is loyal to you, be loyal back. This includes letting him take credit for his successes, but it also means that you take responsibility for his failures. If an employee makes a mistake that angers a client, I tell the client it's my fault. Never, ever blame it on an employee. Blaming an employee for a mistake, even if it *is* his mistake, makes you look small. It's belittling and disgusting. In the end, the buck stops here. It's my name on the front door, my name on the lease, and my name on the paychecks. I hand-picked these people, I hired them, I trained them myself, and I trusted them with a job assignment. So when push comes to shove, it *is* my fault!

> In the end, the buck stops here. It's my name on the front door, my name on the lease, and my name on the paychecks.

The moral of the story: Do not squash an employee's creativity because your own ego won't allow him to have a piece of the success pie. Move aside and give him a little breathing room. Let him show you what he's got, and his talents will come shining through. When your employee takes a chance and does something a little different and creative, encourage him. If he's successful, congratulate him and let him take all the credit. A little praise goes a long way.

If he fails — oh, well! The only way to discover what people are good at is to allow them to try and fail. If your employee knows that his achievements will go unrecognized and that his failures will be criticized, he'll never try anything new and you'll never discover his hidden talents.

HERBISM: IF ALL YOU EVER DO IS TOOT YOUR OWN HORN, YOU'LL NEVER BE ABLE TO CONDUCT THE ORCHESTRA.

29
REIGNING OVER
OFFICE POLITICS

(CONTROLLING GOSSIP AND BACKBITING)

O ver the course of my career as a business owner, there have been times I felt more like a baby-sitter than an entrepreneur. And when I get together with my peers for a drink after hours, more often than not the conversation revolves around which employee caused the biggest migraine that day. It's an ugly fact of business life: if you have employees, you have office politics.

Don't think for a minute that if you own a small business you can avoid the trials and tribulations of office politics. If anything, small offices have it the worst. I'm not sure why, but it seems to be a law of nature. The obvious question is, how do you reduce or eliminate the friction between employees?

TEAM CHEMISTRY

For that answer I turn to sports, particularly college basketball. You see, here in Tucson we aren't big enough for big-time professional sports, so the University of Arizona is king. We have great teams in nearly everything, and if I may brag for a moment, U of A was recently voted the top sports school in the country. However, of all our great teams, basketball is without a doubt the leader. Coach Lute Olson is the most popular man in town, and with good reason. His teams are both dependably terrific and classy. There's always strong chemistry among the teammates.

So how does Lute Olson do it in a sport populated by prima donnas who expect to make millions in the NBA? The secret lies in his approach to recruiting. When Coach Olson considers a new player, he makes sure the potential recruit spends time with the team, testing their chemistry. No chemistry, no scholarship. This technique, though it doesn't guarantee success, is as close to foolproof as you can get.

Translating this to business is easy. Although no one but you (at least while you're starting out) should make any final hiring or firing decisions, letting the existing staff have their say helps smooth out office politics. So when hiring a new employee, I like to involve the rest of my staff. I actually have other employees conduct the initial screening. This not only saves

When hiring a new employee, I like to involve the rest of my staff.

me time and aggravation, it helps create a list of prospective employees who ought to be acceptable to everybody. I conduct the final interviews and cast the deciding vote. Even then, I run it by my staff for discussion before making the job offer. It's my decision, but I share the responsibility with others.

No matter how good your hiring process and office guidelines, I promise you that, as an entrepreneur, office politics could easily be your biggest headache, day in and day out. So

136 what do you do when things start to get out of hand? First, let's look at some potential causes, starting with ego.

THE PRIMA DONNA

The oversized ego of an employee is the most common problem. The old employee resents the new one and feels threatened. Exercise your leadership here. Take the disgruntled employee aside and reassure him that he is of great value to you. Never assume that he knows this. Tell him often. At the same time, be firm and establish that you will not tolerate the sowing of discontent. After all, you spend as much time at the office as you do anywhere else. If it's in upheaval, that just creates stress on you. Uneasy lies the head on which rests the crown.

Uneasy lies the head on which rests the crown.

Another problem is that, in small companies, familiarity often breeds contempt. It's easy for an employee to start thinking of himself as irreplaceable. He can get a bit imperious and start figuratively shoving other employees around. You must take him aside and remind him, as Charles DeGaulle once said when asked how France could survive without him, that the cemeteries are full of men who couldn't be replaced. You were there before your employee, and you will survive long after he's gone. Sounds harsh, I know, but believe me when I tell you that if you're not resolute in this, you'll pay the price later in stress.

Also beware the employee you've promoted who grows drunk with power. A person does not automatically know how to be a good boss. My tip to you is to limit his power at first, especially when it comes to personnel decisions, and to patiently teach him that he can catch more flies with honey than with vinegar.

PROCRASTINATE AND PAY

I've saved the most important thing for last: Do not put off handling office politics. If you think that things will work themselves out, you are wrong, plain and simple. If I sound a little hard or cynical here, forgive me. I have long fought this battle, and to be honest, I still deal with it frequently.

One last hint: In addition to everything I've shared with you so far, I also try to draw my employees into an extended family of sorts. I regularly conduct "office symposiums," which is our code for spending an afternoon goofing off at the movies. And from time to time I take the whole staff and their spouses to my house at the beach for a weekend of sun and fun. And, of course, there are the customary Christmas, New Year's, and birthday parties.

Make office harmony a top priority, and you'll reap the rewards in reduced stress.

HERBISM: BE AN ENLIGHTENED MONARCH: TREAT YOUR EMPLOYEES LIKE MEMBERS OF PARLIAMENT, BUT KEEP THE FINAL DECISIONS FOR YOURSELF.

30
SHORT GOOD-BYES

(WHEN THEY ABSOLUTELY, POSITIVELY HAVE TO GO)

I **would sooner pluck out my** nose hairs one by one than fire somebody, but sometimes an employee leaves you with no alternative.

Let me back up for a second and tell you when *not* to fire someone. You can't fire someone for breaking a rule she didn't know existed. For example, you can't fire your assistant because she showed up with a spike through her tongue if she didn't know that visible body piercings are against company policy — regardless of how obvious you may think it is. It's common sense to you because it's your business. You can't assume others automatically see things the way you do.

The solution? An employee manual. I don't care if you run a two-person company, you should always provide a manual outlining the dos and don'ts of your corporate policies. I'm not talking an eighty-page dissertation — just a couple of pages clearly stating what you expect from your employees and what you will offer in return. "Work starts at nine in the morning and ends at six in the evening, with one hour for lunch beginning at noon. Punctuality is mandatory, as is professional attire. Paychecks are distributed on the first and fifteenth of every month. Work-related purchases must be approved in advance by the office manager and will be reimbursed to the purchaser five working days after the receipt has been handed to the office manager." You get the idea. No issue is too insignificant. Most people aren't mind readers. If you don't tell them, how are they supposed to know?

THE BITTER END

For all the credit and praise I've given employees, I know that sometimes you end up with a lost cause — a person you've worked with, offered different positions to, and been very patient with, but who just doesn't seem to work out well. These are what I call "employees beyond redemption." As much as I support flexibility, no matter how hard you bang the hammer, a square peg is never going to fit into a round hole.

> No matter how hard you bang the hammer, a square peg will never fit into a round hole.

But before you give an employee the old heave-ho, there are a couple of things you must do to forestall a wrongful dismissal suit: warn and document. If she crosses the line or disregards an aspect of company policy outlined in your employee manual, publicly recognize her mistake then and there. If your receptionist returns from lunch twenty minutes late, warn her that extended lunch breaks are not tolerated. If a customer sales rep shows up wearing jeans, make it clear that the dress code outlined in the employee manual will be strictly enforced.

I'm human, just like everybody else. We all have our bad days, and we all make mistakes. That's why these are warnings.

140 A single instance is one thing, but a recurring disregard for company policy is entirely another. You must draw the line somewhere.

COVER YOUR BUTT

As far as documenting is concerned, keep files on all your employees. Use it to record their actions, both positive and negative. If an employee continuously stays late for two weeks trying to finish an important project for the company, make a note of her strong work ethic and devotion to her job. If your secretary habitually returns late from lunch, make a note of her tardiness each time, as well as the fact that you spoke to her on each occasion about adhering to company policy. Of course, the contents of these files are completely confidential, as is their existence. They're for your eyes only, and if necessary, your lawyer's.

If it gets to the point where an employee has blatantly ignored company policies and your repeated warnings, off with his head! I'm only half-joking; that's really the way you have to treat it, like a beheading. The faster you do it, the neater and less painful it will be for everyone. Does that sound heartless? It isn't. Look, as I said earlier, I hate firing employees. I avoid it at all costs, and when I know I'll have to do it, it bothers me for days before and after. I've tried being nice and sympathetic, and it only makes it worse. Forget the long speeches and the Hallmark cards. It's like a Band-Aid: the faster you rip it off, the less it hurts.

TIME TO CUT BAIT

So you've warned. You've documented. You've torn your hair out trying to avoid it, but you have to fire someone. Here's what you do. You walk right up to the person with a check for two weeks' salary in your hand. You hand her the check and say, "You're fired. Clear out your desk." No need for explanations. She's had plenty of warnings; this should not be a surprise. And no matter how fair you've been to her, she's going to dislike you intensely at this moment. Trying to make her feel good at this point only adds insult to injury.

Just watch her as she clears out her desk, then escort her out. And as much as I hate to say it, have a witness present throughout. It may be uncomfortable, but you can't be too careful these days about sexual harassment and wrongful dismissal suits. In the end, it's your butt on the line.

HERBISM: "YOU'RE FIRED. CLEAN OUT YOUR DESK." IT'S TOUGH, BUT IT'S THE ONLY WAY.

31
LEADING BY REMOTE CONTROL

(RELAX, BUT KEEP AN EYE ON THINGS)

So now you're the big cheese, having more fun than you ever thought possible, and all because you realized that you're an entrepreneur, not a hands-on manager. Congratulations! You're way ahead of the pack. This is the one ability that separates the big successes from the small ones.

However, now you have a whole new problem. How do you keep your finger on your company's pulse without becoming a meddler and undermining the very lifestyle you labored to create? This is important, because just as you must know when to let go of the day-to-day details, you must also know how to protect your interests. If you don't, at the very least you'll end up in the middle of a mess; at worst, you'll be stolen blind.

Such is the way of the world. And it happens to the best of 143 us. Ralph Ellison, founder of giant Oracle Corporation, was off enjoying his sailboat when he suddenly discovered his company's stock diving because of disappointing profits, the result of bad management. He had to drop what he was doing and get back in. The story has a happy ending, though. He learned in a big way what I am about to teach you, and balance was restored, both at Oracle and with Ralph.

HIRE A GOOD MANAGER

It's very simple, really. First, you need to pick the best person you can to be your manager. Most of the time, a good, old-fashioned MBA "suit" will do the job, but sometimes a seasoned manager with a lot of business background will do it better. The most important thing is that he or she "gets it" — that is, understands what it is about your company that makes it unique. Take your time picking this person, and after winnowing down your choices, as with any other employee, make sure that your new top manager understands that you're still the boss.

Once you've hired, you've got to give your manager lots of room to run, but with oversight. This simply means having a system for keeping abreast of the big picture. Here's how you can do it easily. First, remember that budget we talked about? Well, it's more useful in this role than it ever was in starting up your venture. Every year, you need to sit down with your manager or department heads and draw up a budget. Let them come up with their own numbers for each expense category as well as revenue projections.

> **The most important thing is that your manager understands what makes your company unique.**

Then grit your teeth (the tedium of meetings is something few entrepreneurs can stand!) and have a meeting to discuss each category and amount of income and outgo and debate the numbers until everyone agrees they're good.

GET DETAILED REPORTS

Each month, have a detailed cash flow report generated from your accounting system. Your accountant will have long since set you up with one, or you can buy any number of computer applications like Quicken or Peachtree (just to name a couple). In a meeting with your manager, go over each category and check it against your budget. If there are significant differences, discuss them. Either adjust the budget to accommodate them or implement a fix for the problem. Ask your manager to report also on personnel matters, marketing plans, competition, regulatory changes, new technologies — in short, everthing that could affect the health of your company.

Instead of being chief cook and bottle washer, you're the head honcho.

The most important thing to remember here is that you are still the Admiral of the Fleet. It's your battle plan, your vision that gives the company its uniqueness. Never believe that anyone you hire could do your job. If she could, she would have started a company of her own. And in many businesses, the customers assume that you are still in charge. Now, however, instead of being chief cook and bottle washer, you're the head honcho.

SET THE COURSE

You still have the last word on future direction and strategic planning. You will still originate lots of creative ideas. Though it is just plain smart to include your employees and managers in the creative process, it is important to remember not to give the keys to a stranger and hit the high seas. You're giving up driving, not road trips. You're hiring a chauffeur and sitting in the back.

This is the only realistic way to make time for great sex. The business is yours, baby! You conceived it, nurtured it, and watched it grow into maturity. It's probably unrealistic to think that you would or could abandon it, short of selling it, to someone else. However, just as with a child, to make sure it grows strong and healthy you have to let it find its own way. At the same time, you should never completely take your eyes off it. The trick is in the balance.

HERBISM: DELEGATE, DON'T ABDICATE!

32
KNOW WHEN TO FOLD 'EM

(HELLO — YOUR FIFTEEN MINUTES OF FAME ARE UP)

As thrilling as personal success can be, don't forget that all glory is fleeting. Businesses and their owners all have their day in the sun, but it can't be sunshiny all the time. There comes a point when all business owners must either close their doors or pass the baton, based on one of the following three scenarios:

- You failed.
- Your success is marginal.
- You want to cash in your chips.

FAILURE IS NOT THE END

Let's start with the first and most humbling of the three scenarios: failure. Without a doubt, the worst part of failure is accepting it. But if you learn to read the writing on the wall, the hardest part is over. Admitting failure is tough. Moving on is easy!

In order to gauge your business's success, you must constantly evaluate your profits and your expenses. However, be careful not to judge your business too quickly or too harshly. The first six months of a business's life are considered its infancy, and what happens then doesn't tell you much about how well you'll do in the long run. Your business must adjust itself to its surroundings, and the surroundings must get to know your business.

However, there comes a point in your business plan when the numbers should start to fall into line with your expectations. Somewhere in your 12-, 24-, or 36-month projections, the numbers are supposed to begin improving steadily, and revenues should begin to exceed expenses. If what's happening doesn't look much like your plan, you've got a problem.

If your business is a new product or service that doesn't seem to have caught on yet, it's probably never going to. Some concepts just will not sell, regardless of how diligently you research, how hard you work, or how desperately you want to succeed. If it doesn't grab the public right away, chances are it never will.

> Some concepts just will not sell, regardless of how diligently you research, how hard you work, or how desperately you want to succeed.

Now, if you've opened a business that's a variation on an existing, successful business theme — such as an ice cream parlor or a clothing store — and the public doesn't seem to be responding, it can mean one of two things: either the public doesn't like your approach to the business — products, services, location —

148 or your marketing campaign is all wrong. Both of these problems are fixable. But if you fiddle with them and business still doesn't pick up, it's time to throw in the white towel before your business's blood starts running in the street.

When my pet stores failed, I saw it coming about three months in advance but didn't know how to fix it. Sales were slacking off. Inventory was thin. We couldn't afford to keep the stores as snazzy as they should have been kept. Like a lot of first-time entrepreneurs, I was in denial. I didn't want to accept that my empire was crumbling.

I fell victim to the "Yes, buts." My advisors warned me again and again that the end was near, but I always had a response. "Yes, but once the marketing campaign picks up speed, business will be great." Or "Yes, but if we just have one really good month, we can make up for the last three." Once you start playing this catch-up game, the game is over.

"If your outgo exceeds your income, the upkeep will be your downfall."

Years ago someone shared with me an old saying that is the absolute core to understanding when your business has had it: "If your outgo exceeds your income, the upkeep will be your downfall." Look, folks, old sayings are old sayings because they're true. Don't fool yourself into believing that you're going to be the exception to the rule, because you will be sorely disappointed. It's as dependable as the law of gravity: if your costs exceed your revenues after the initial, planned start-up period, keeping your doors open will send you straight into bankruptcy. There's no fancy way to put it. If the numbers are going down instead of up, you're failing. You have to just accept it.

Businesses do not go bankrupt all by themselves. They go bankrupt because their owners can't bring themselves to accept failure. So instead of quitting while they still have the skin on their backs, they drag it out until the business is dead ten times over and there's nothing they can do to fix it. Then they have to file for bankruptcy because it's the only way out. If you recognize ahead of time that your business is going down the tubes, you can still save yourself from going bankrupt. Refusing to admit failure because you cannot swallow your pride is the most destructive thing you can do.

So here's how you handle it: If the writing is on the wall and you know it's just a matter of time before your business goes belly-up, get out while you still have something left to negotiate with. Sell anything you can — inventory, capital, fixtures — and use that cash to appease your creditors. If you approach them with honesty and willingly explain that your business isn't succeeding and that you're calling it quits, you'd be surprised how many of them will work with you to settle your debts.

Creditors are people, too; generally speaking, they will help you avoid bankruptcy at all costs. They know that if you go bankrupt, they get nothing. And since something is always better than nothing, nine times out of ten they will work out a payment plan to slowly absolve your debt. If you're obliged to pay $1,500 a month for rent, negotiate your way out of your lease; promise to pay $400 a month over a longer period to keep your track record clean. I guarantee that your landlord would rather get $400 a month for the next two years than nothing at all. And your credit rating stays good because you didn't have to file for bankruptcy! It's a win-win situation.

GETTING OUT OF THE DOLDRUMS

The second scenario for calling it quits is achieving steady, marginal success. Entrepreneurs often find themselves staying afloat, but not by very much. When this happens, it's time to go back to the drawing board. Reevaluate your situation. Analyze your business strategy, marketing plan, and product or service. Ask yourself, "What can I do to improve this? Could I increase my marketing budget? Broaden my product line? Change my presentation?" If you find something you can do to improve your business's performance, jump in with both feet and do it.

If you decide there's nothing you can do to increase revenue, it becomes a quality-of-life judgment call. Is it worth it to you to sit in a marginally successful business for the rest of your

150 life, making just enough money to get by without any hope of improving? I suspect not.

The solution? Sell. Call up a business broker, put the word out that you're selling, and see what kind of offers you get. Marginally successful businesses tend to sell well. A lot of entrepreneurs prefer fixer-uppers to brand new businesses, so it shouldn't be long before you get an offer. Take the money and run. Then — after you've analyzed your almost-success — go back to the drawing board and try something else.

DANGER: SUCCESS!

The third scenario is the ideal for an entrepreneur. Business is booming. The phone is ringing nonstop. Customers are pouring through the doors. Revenue is skyrocketing off the charts. You've got so much business you don't know what to do with it all! Warning: Even though you are having the time of your life, you are now entering a danger zone.

Of course, you can avoid entering this zone by selling now. If it's easy to unload a going concern that hasn't reached its potential, it's positively a cinch to cash in a successful one. Collect the big bucks, move to Hawaii, and sip Lava Flows beneath the swaying coconut palms.

Most successful entrepreneurs, however, never figure to retire. If, like me, you're one of those, read on, because the biggest mistake you can make in this situation is not recognizing when you have exercised your talents to their fullest. You see, as the company grows, there will be more and more people on board and acres of technical issues to deal with: meetings, long-term business plans, expanding into new markets, employee benefits — all sorts of stuff. When you're sitting in a meeting and your staff is discussing important details like cash-flow planning, tax issues, employee benefit programs, and extended budgets, and you

Cash-flow planning, tax issues, employee benefit programs — this is not what you became an entrepreneur for!

feel your eyes glaze over and roll back in your head — this is not what you became an entrepreneur for!

It's time to hire a president and become chairperson of the board. There's a huge difference between the skills of an entrepreneur and those of an MBA. Entrepreneurs are creative and ambitious; MBAs tend to be cautious and attentive to detail. Remember the filthy, stinking rich lifestyle: time to pursue fun outside the office! Last I checked, projecting the next four years' biquarterly earnings and studying tax-planning benefits in depth is not fun. You need to stay aboard as your company's creative fountainhead, but you do not — I repeat — you do not need to be involved in life-force-sucking details. Bring in the suits, and go play golf!

HERBISM: WHEN YOU REACH YOUR FIFTEENTH MINUTE OF FAME, CASH IN YOUR CHIPS AND HAVE A PARTY!

PART IV

MAKE TIME FOR GREAT SEX

(...and Other Important Things in Life)

33
THE SEX METAPHOR

(THE REAL PLEASURES OF BIG MONEY)

Let me clarify this once and for all: This book is not really about sex. "Having time for great sex" is a metaphor for anything you enjoy doing away from the office — acts that are fulfilling and bring you joy but that don't make you money. Participating in sports with your friends, spending time with your children, shopping, going on vacation — and, yes, having great sex.

Let's be honest. Money is the biggest cause of stress in most people's lives. It hangs over their heads, determining how they live their lives, dictating what they can and cannot do. Stop for a minute and imagine what your life would be like if you never

156 had to think about money. Being able to go wherever you want, whenever you want, and do whatever you want — without ever thinking about how much it costs. It boggles the mind.

FLASH: MONEY CAN BUY FREEDOM!

There's a wildly misguided notion floating around American society that rich people aren't happy, that their wealth is a burden. Let me take this opportunity to demolish that myth. As I asserted in the opening chapter, you can be pretty damn happy with a few million bucks. Not because money can buy you happiness, but because having money allows you the freedom to do whatever it is that makes you happy.

Yesterday, which was Wednesday, I spent the morning at the office, then met my best friend for lunch. After that I had a workout with my personal trainer. Then I headed home early and went for a bike ride with my kids, during other people's working hours. Now, that bike ride didn't cost a nickel, but think of how luxurious it was to be able to take it. I could have done any number of things that cost a big wad of cash, but that's not the point. I wanted to spend the afternoon riding a bike around the neighborhood with my kids, and that's just what I did. That's the luxury that wealth affords me. It's what being filthy, stinking rich and still having time for great sex is all about.

You can be pretty damn happy with a few million bucks.

HERBISM: "GREAT SEX" IS THE LUXURY OF DOING WHAT YOU WANT, WHEN YOU WANT.

34

BEING THERE

(ALL TIME IS QUALITY TIME)

The biggest mistake most people make trying to get rich is spending more time at the office. They think the more time they spend at work, the more money they'll make, and that the more money they make, the happier they'll ultimately be.

I have a news flash for you, folks: Becoming a fanatical, obsessed, stressed-out workaholic in order to make a lot of money is not going to make you happy. It's going to make you a fanatical, obsessed, stressed-out, miserable jerk.

Putting in unnecessary overtime at the office is a self-destructive habit. Nothing will ruin your life more quickly than an unwavering focus on your career with total neglect of your personal life. The whole point of having more money is to be able to afford more free time to spend with family, friends, and hobbies. What's the point of it all if you're at the office late

158 every night and on the weekends? Each week of your life that you spend as a workaholic is a week of your life that you've wasted.

WHAT'S REALLY IMPORTANT?

Workaholism is when you and your occupation become indistinguishable, and what you do becomes who you are. All workaholics live in La-La Land and think that workaholism is normal. Twelve-hour days, seven-day work-weeks, years devoid of vacations — these are things that inspire pride in the hearts of workaholics. Does anyone else notice how whacked that mentality is?

I am all for hard work, but there's a line that needs to be drawn. This is about being able to recognize and prioritize what's really important in your life. For some people, it's God first, family second, themselves third. Others put themselves before all. That's not my department. If you want advice on that, ask your rabbi, priest, minister, guru, or shrink. But what I can tell you is that work is never, ever first on *my* list. If career tops your list of life's priorities, you've got problems.

If career tops your list of life's priorities, you've got problems.

I know, because I've been there. When I began my career, I did none of the things I espouse now. I was employed by someone else, and I was a total workaholic. Later, after my first business failed, I was so afraid it might happen again that I worked around the clock, day in and day out. At the time I was in insurance, and later investing, working on commission only. Talk about uptight!

Then one day about eight years ago I had an epiphany. I was on vacation with my wife and kids at Disney World — the first vacation I had taken in years, and boy, did I go begrudgingly! I was being dragged around Epcot Center, pouting all the while because I hadn't talked to the office in two whole hours, when suddenly I received an urgent page. I frantically shoved my family onto the monorail and hurried them to the nearest hotel, where I proceeded to sit in the basement, talking on a pay phone until I had the incident worked out to my satisfaction.

When I finally emerged — three and a half hours later — my wife was in a cold fury. "Herb, you've been in this business for twelve years. If after all that time you've built yourself a business that's going to disintegrate because you're not there twenty-four hours a day, then you haven't built a business at all." And that was it. The lightbulb went on over my head, and I stood there stupefied, thinking, "What the hell am I doing?"

LET GOOD THINGS HAPPEN

Control is an illusion. You cannot expect to control your business's every move. What's going to happen is going to happen, no matter how much you fret over it. Now, of course you can take the obvious steps by hiring an efficient staff and training them well. But beyond that, there's not much you can do. "Oopses" and "Uh-ohs" happen. They just do.

What I found, and what you will find, is that the more you relax, the more efficiently you'll work. You may think you hide your tension well, but you don't. It comes through in everything you do, and your family, friends, and employees react to it. Believe me, people work and play better with those who don't raise their anxiety level. Relax — and it will rub off on your co-workers and customers.

People work and play better with those who don't raise their anxiety level.

One more thing: this whole quality versus quantity time thing is nonsense. Time is time. You cannot categorize it. There's no such thing as quality time that isn't quantity time. Your very presence with the people you love is what matters most. Your child doesn't think, "Boy, I can't wait for Daddy to come home so we can have fifteen minutes of quality time playing catch in the backyard after dinner and before bedtime!" Your husband doesn't think, "I can't wait for my wife to get home so we can hurry to the grocery store together and get in one hour of shopping before it closes!"

160 Your kids, your spouse, your friends, your family — they just want to hang out with you. It doesn't really matter what you do during that time, but the more of it there is, the better. Being filthy, stinking rich is having an abundance of time to spend with the people you love, and quantity is quality.

HERBISM: RELAX. LIFE'S JUST TOO SHORT, BABY.

35

LEAVE WORK AT WORK

(DO IT RIGHT, THEN GET LOST)

There's an evil rumor circulating in the business world that the harder you work, the more you make. Bullshit! It's not how hard you work, it's how smart you work. In order to be happy, you have to have the time to be happy. And in order to have the time to be happy, you have to manage your time effectively. That means spending less than eighty hours a week at your desk.

TIME MANAGEMENT 101

There are four cardinal rules for managing your time at the office effectively. Rule number one is simple: When you go to the office to work, work. Just for the record, reading the paper is not working. Milling around the water

162 cooler with co-workers is not working. Lunching with your buddies is not working.

Here's how I work: Come into the office first thing in the morning. Prioritize what I have to do. Do it. Do it immediately. Do not pass Go. Do not fool around. Do not call my friends. Do my work. Go home when I'm finished.

You'll be amazed how much you can accomplish in a short time when you stay focused. And when you do finish early, don't feel guilty and look for other things to do. Go home and relax!

This doesn't mean you can't socialize with your employees. Go to happy hour when the workday is over. I'm friendly with every one of my employees, but we don't play during business hours. We work. When the work is done, we socialize.

Never impose deadlines on yourself that will require you to work extra hours.

Rule number two: Never impose deadlines on yourself that will require you to work extra hours, unless that commitment is vital to your business's survival. When promising a customer a product or service, estimate how much time it would take you to deliver it if everything went exactly right and you had no distractions. Double it. Then add 20 percent. If you think you can do it in two days, tell him five. That way you can be confident that you will keep your word. And if you get it done early, the customer will think the world of you. Then you can move on to the next project without stress!

GET AWAY FROM IT ALL

Rule number three: Learn how to take a vacation. Sounds silly, doesn't it? You'd be surprised how many people can't do this. When you're on vacation, do not call the office. I repeat: Do not call the office. This was a hard one for me to learn. I have ruined more than one vacation in a state of unsubstantiated panic. But ever since I mastered "vacation let-go," my life has been much easier. The solution is easy: e-mail.

Check it once a day. And be very careful not to commit the 163 biggest of all vacation fouls: convincing yourself that a business trip is a vacation. No way! There's no relaxation involved in a working vacation. It's all the same stresses of the office, just with a change of scenery.

Rule number four: Don't go to sleep with it. Two in the morning is that hellish time when problems seem monumental because it's too late to fix them — so do the best thing you can: forget about them. When you leave the office, leave the work behind. Personal time is not personal time if you spend it thinking about work. The only thing you should be thinking about when you go to bed at night is the sound of your own breathing. The office will still be there when you wake up tomorrow.

HERBISM: WORK IS WORK. PERSONAL TIME IS PERSONAL TIME. NEVER THE TWAIN SHOULD MEET.

36
SHARE WISDOM AND WORRIES

(MENTORS AND PEER CONFIDANTS)

Besides family and co-workers, there are two types of relationships that are close to the heart of this entrepreneur: mentoring and peer confidants. One is unique to the position of being an entrepreneur. The other is something that everyone should have.

THE WISDOM OF THE MASTER

Anyone who knows me knows that I love mentoring. It is perhaps the best part about being a successful entrepreneur. By mentoring, you give someone an opportunity that will positively affect his life — the opportunity to benefit from your experience and accumulated wisdom. This is an opportunity that he would not otherwise have had, because no one else can pass along to him what you uniquely know.

Mentoring covers a lot of ground. Whenever you hire an intern, offer advice to a less experienced operator, or invest in the business of a promising first-time entrepreneur, you're mentoring. You're accessing your business skills and successes to further the career of another. It's an act of great generosity. But "generous" doesn't mean "selfless." You gain the satisfaction of having helped someone, and that's no small reward. You will probably get referral business from grateful students. It can be a hell of a lot of fun. Besides — admit it — your ego enjoys the respect and admiration you get from your juniors.

A SHOULDER TO CRY ON

A peer confidant is the kind of friend everyone should have, but one that an entrepreneur cannot live without. A peer confidant is a friend upon whom you can unload your every concern and problem without worrying about how it's going to affect his life. For me, it's my best friend, Mark. You see, when you're running your own business, you experience all sorts of victories and losses, some big, some little, that weigh on your mind — things you'll want to unload on a willing ear.

> A peer confidant is a person everyone should have, but one that an entrepreneur cannot live without.

Your spouse or significant other is not an option, nor is a co-worker. Their lives are directly intertwined with yours, and some of these worries are not things that you need to disclose to them. I'm sure you've had the kind of worries (I have them all the time!) that seem gargantuan to you until you talk about them with someone else. Giving voice to your worries can put them in perspective and help you realize they aren't really catastrophic, after all.

Mark is the ideal peer confidant for me. Not only is he a good friend, he's an entrepreneur as well, so he understands

166 where I'm coming from. We meet for lunch and swap business concerns. Sometimes there's advice-giving, but more often than not we just listen to each other. Then I go home and he goes home, and we don't dwell on each other's problems. You could never do that with your family or employees without making them worry about where their next meal is coming from! To stay grounded, every entrepreneur needs a peer confidant.

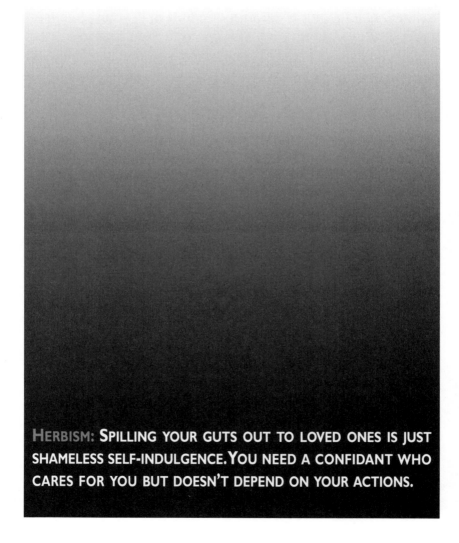

HERBISM: SPILLING YOUR GUTS OUT TO LOVED ONES IS JUST SHAMELESS SELF-INDULGENCE. YOU NEED A CONFIDANT WHO CARES FOR YOU BUT DOESN'T DEPEND ON YOUR ACTIONS.

37
CHANNEL YOUR AMBITION

(KNOW WHEN TO STOP BEING A HERO)

Perhaps the two most admirable qualities of an entrepreneur are ambition and courage. Without these attributes, no entrepreneur would ever succeed. However, if you're not careful, these strengths can easily be warped and twisted into weaknesses.

SUCCESS FUEL

Ambition is the key to being successful. It's the get-up-and-go that keeps you moving. But there are two kinds of ambition: driving and consuming. Driving is the good kind; consuming ambition will suck your life force. Driving

168 ambition motivates you without overtaking you. It empowers you to campaign diligently for your business plan and raise every last cent of the necessary capital. It keeps you determined to uphold the highest quality of product or service. It leads you to thoroughly research and plan your marketing strategy. Driving ambition is a very good thing!

Your ambition can be strong without being consuming.

But entrepreneurs can easily be consumed by ambition. They become insatiable, hungrily working toward one lofty goal after another. Being consumingly ambitious is a hollow life — it's the life of a workaholic, devoid of personal aspirations. Consumingly ambitious people put their work-related goals and obligations above all else. They tear through life with blinders on, oblivious to anything beyond the confines of their business.

Ambition is great. Make it a positive force that keeps you moving and helps you deal with the inevitable bumps in the business road, but keep it reined in. Your ambition can be strong without being consuming.

LONELY ARE THE BRAVE

Courage is another quality high on the entrepreneur's menu of virtues. Starting your own business means taking a big risk with the quality of your life. You're putting your financial future on the line. Of course you need courage to forge ahead! But courageous, ambitious people are often mistaken for egomaniacs, when actually the two are completely unrelated.

Look, I know I'm great at what I do, and knowing my own abilities gives me the strength to carry on when times are bad. That's courage. Thinking that my abilities make me better than someone else? That's egomania. There's nothing wrong with acknowledging your skills. Pretending that you're not good at what you're good at is phony humility — and that's disgusting.

Courageous people are secure in their abilities, which makes them confident individuals. To be honest, less successful and

less confident people will often try to pull you down by accusing 169
you of being an egomaniac. Misery loves company. Ignore it!

There's a big, big difference between being courageous and being egomaniacal. An egomaniac is a person who needs to parade his talents up and down the street and put other people down in order to feel good about himself. And that's certainly not your style, is it?

HERBISM: BE AMBITIOUS. BE COURAGEOUS. BUT DON'T BE A JERK!

38
WHEN YOU'VE GOT IT, FLAUNT IT

(PLEASE YOUR FANS, SCREW YOUR ENEMIES)

Bad news, folks: the road to becoming wealthy is not the road to being loved by all. The more successful you become, the more people you will inevitably alienate along the way, through no fault of your own. As your success grows, the people you know will begin to fall into three general categories: groupies, enemies, and conquests. Hey — you can't please everybody!

ALLIES AND ANTAGONISTS

The first and most important group of people consists of your fans. These are your loyal friends and relatives who want nothing but the best for you. You can — for the most part — do no wrong in their eyes. They love you, they love

that you're successful, they love watching you in action — the 171
whole kit and caboodle. I'm half-joking when I call them your
groupies, but in a way that's what they are: your unwavering
support team. My wife actually coined the term. She calls
herself and the kids "Herby's Groupies." Cute, isn't it?

Next in line are your enemies, or as I like to call them, the
anti-groupies. These people don't like you — at all — but they
can't really put their finger on
why. Most of them don't know
you well enough to pass judgment on your character, but
that doesn't stop them from
doing so. These are the people
you briefly brush up against in
life and later find out they hate
you, but you have no idea what

> **There's no way to rise to the top without defeating the competition, but that doesn't mean they're going to like you.**

on earth you did to make them dislike you. I'll tell you their
motivation: envy. Just like the bully on the elementary school
playground, your enemies criticize you only because they're
jealous of your success, plain and simple.

The third and final group are also your enemies. They're
your conquests, the business competitors you beat. There's no
way to rise to the top without defeating the competition — it's
an inevitable part of success — but that doesn't mean they're
going to like you for it.

TO EACH HIS OWN

My advice on how to juggle these opposing groups? Play
to your fans and screw your enemies. You're not running for president; don't go around kissing babies and
schmoozing with strangers. You can't please everybody, and you
shouldn't want to. Trying to be everyone's friend will compro-
mise your individuality, which is the worst thing you can do
to yourself.

You have to live your life for yourself and those you love,
and forget about everyone else. Do what you want, paying
attention only to your groupies: your spouse or significant

172 other, kids if you have them, a few close friends, and some trusted associates. Who else do you need? No one.

Dudes and dudettes, listen carefully to this. Don't change your tune to try to win over your anti-groupies and conquests. If you to try to make everyone happy, you'll end up making no one happy. It will only add stress to your life.

If you're successful, don't pretend you're not. If you want to buy your wife the BMW, buy your wife the BMW. If you want to buy your husband the super-monster-sized entertainment system to watch the games on, buy it. If you want to send your kids to an Ivy League school, send them. If you work hard and can afford it, spend your money on anything you want! Don't worry about what your enemies and conquests think of you. Yes, these are the trappings of wealth that we hear so much about. But what I want to know is, what's the good of being wealthy if you don't have a few trappings?

HERBISM: GO AHEAD — BE OSTENTATIOUS, AND ENJOY EVERY MINUTE OF IT!

39

WE ARE ALL SINNERS

(BUT THAT'S NO EXCUSE)

When you are successful in business, it rapidly becomes clear that it's good to be King (or Queen)! Having a lot of money can bring many wonderful things. But what about the pitfalls? When you become filthy, stinking rich, new opportunities, experiences, choices, and temptations will be thrown continually into your path, and it's easy to lose perspective.

It's also easy to make a mess of everything that you have so painstakingly built. The greatest dangers in life are not financial; what brings most of us down in the end are the self-destructive things we do in our private lives. Money and power can bring out the worst in any of us. Believe me, I know. Remember that ruined marriage I told you about?

When you're sitting on top, keeping your moral compass pointed north can be difficult. Everyone knows about the obvious traps — drugs, alcohol, gambling — but what about sex?

DRIVE, HE SAID

Let's start with a simple observation: Particularly in the case of men, ambition and sex drive are all wound up together. The more ambitious the man, the more sexually aggressive he will be. Period. I think that it is some sort of testosterone thing. There are no exceptions to this, and if you think that you know someone who is somehow different, trust me, you don't know him as well as you think you do.

There are lots of studies done about sex drive and fantasies, and all kinds of kinky stuff. One recent poll stated that the average man sexually fantasizes about eight times a day. Well, I'm here to tell you that the guys they polled either lied because they thought their wives would find out what they said, or they were a bunch of eunuchs. Speaking for myself, I can say with authority that I fantasize about eight times an hour!

Speaking for myself, I can say with authority that I fantasize about eight times an hour!

And ladies, speaking as a man who did more than his share of casual dating, I can say with some authority that your sex drives are pretty much a man's equal, if perhaps more surreptitious. I have been out with more than one woman who has been the seducer rather than the seduced, and who, as I got to know them better, shared with me sexual fantasies that were, how shall I put this delicately, well developed and very explicit.

YOUR CHEATIN' HEART

There is, however, a big difference between men and women in the reasons they cheat on their partners. Men cheat because they do. They're just being men. They have an innate need to populate the planet. Women cheat because they are made to feel unattractive by their spouse or partner. And both cheat because of the dirty little secret of many marriages: Tie the knot; say goodbye to your sex life as you once knew it.

Oh, I know I'm going to get a lot of angry reactions to this 175 one, but if that weren't true, there wouldn't be literally thousands of books written on how to spice up your crappy married sex life. Bookstores stock only what sells. Let me save you some time and money in understanding this phenomenon as well as the adultery that results.

First, living together, dating forever, screwing like rabbits before marriage, or even abstaining from premarital sex altogether are all fine and dandy as far as they go, but none of

> Take it from experience, a man can forget the name of a women he has been intimate with unless she is real trouble.

them are any sort of rehearsal for marriage or guarantor of later success. They will have no affect whatsoever on your married sex life. The fact is, the reason that sex is great before marriage or in an affair, and so tough afterward, is the danger. You see, when you are not married, you can always walk away — or worse, your partner can. Even if you live together, the threat is always there. And it is there because either you or your mate wants it to be; otherwise you would already be married!

Therefore, always in the back of your mind is the knowledge that if you screw it up, you could wind up alone, and since no one likes to be alone, the element of danger lurks in every nonmarried relationship — hence, great sex! But tie that knot, make it a contract that binds, and baby, danger turns to asphyxiation, and bye-bye sex life as you once knew it. Get it?

Men are always going to cheat more than women for one simple reason: sex is a mostly physical act for them, with the exception of isolated experiences of overwhelming passion that usually occur with women who are either "The One" or no damn good for them. Take it from experience, a man can forget the name of a woman he has been intimate with unless she is real trouble or his future Mrs. He'll remember that girl forever!

What this means is that a man can have an affair and never think of it as anything but fun. This is especially true of ambitious men who are likely to be the most successful in life. Their guilt will not overwhelm them, if they feel it at all. Heck, to a lot of these men, mistresses seem like an entitlement.

176   As a side note, this is the answer to the "smart women, foolish choices" conundrum. Why do great women consistently pick men who are bad for them? Because the very characteristics that make them dogs make them the best providers, namely, drive and ambition. It's just Mother Nature talking. Casper Milquetoast might sound good in theory, but in reality no woman really wants to live like a medieval peasant forever if she can help it. She's looking for Prince Charming, but in the real world the prince is a predator. Hence, she hooks up with Johnny Dangerously. Be honest, girls, if a man is too nice or too attentive, don't you just want to run for the hills?

Back to our discussion of infidelity. While the men are cheating on their wives, those still beautiful women they married are being made to feel pretty damn unattractive. And boys, I'm warning you, some day another fella is going to come along and make her feel like the sexy woman she is. Sir Lancelot is going to show up, King Arthur. Bingo, your wife is having an affair.

MARRIAGE IS GOOD

Let's take a moment right here to set the record straight. Now that I have written what sounds like a Clintonesque litany of excuses for adultery and slammed the hell out of marital sex, I want to say that I think the whole adultery business is absolutely contemptible. It will destroy your family, drive away your friends, and probably lead to the destruction of your business. Therefore, I have a simple piece of advice for you: Don't do it.

> I want to say that I think the whole adultery business is absolutely contemptible.

Folks, I am as pro-marriage and pro-family as they come. Though sex will change in a marriage, it can evolve into something quite beautiful, an expression of love for your life partner. And if you feel your marriage cannot be saved and you don't have kids yet, you can either grow up or get divorced. But once you have those little darlings, you had better put any thought of giving up out of your

head. You are going to screw your kids up as sure as God made
little green apples if you divorce, and that has terrible repercussions not only for them, but for all the rest of society as well. I just love to hear how men and women bent on destroying their marriages always say the kids will be better off because of all the fighting they have to witness in their current situation. Oh, please, save that crock for some idiot who believes it. That is just a selfish excuse.

> **Don't buy into that poverty bullshit. The crime rate didn't budge in the Great Depression.**

Sociologists generally agree with the obvious conclusion that the breakdown of the nuclear family is the primary cause of increased crime and violence in our society. Don't buy into that poverty bullshit. The crime rate didn't budge in the Great Depression, and people were a lot poorer then than they are now, and heavily armed to boot! What was the difference? Families stayed together and pulled through the hard times. Sounds quaint, doesn't it? So much more is the tragedy of what has happened since, but I digress.

LEAD US NOT INTO TEMPTATION

So given all these animal drives and temptations, how do you avoid disaster? Easy. Don't put yourself into a position to be compromised, and nothing can happen. Boy, do I get sick and tired of hearing men and women lament about messing their lives up in affairs, with the excuse that "it just happened." Baloney. Nothing "just happens." Let's see, you were walking down the street with your platonic friend of the opposite sex, a hurricane suddenly blew your clothes off, you both fell to the ground, and your penis and vagina accidentally came together. Yeah, sure.

Here's what always really happens. Two people start with the lie that they are just friends, and they tell this lie even to themselves. Then they start spending time together. A lunch here, an after-work drink there, et cetera, and always with lots of conversation. Over time, the conversation becomes more

178 and more intimate. They start confiding in each other little secrets of how their lives are unhappy one way or another, and the conversation becomes more and more personal from there. Before you know it, they find themselves in a full-blown affair that "just happened."

So, if you never allow yourself intimacy with another person of the opposite sex, you cannot have an affair. This means no meetings with any member of the other team unless in a group, no dinners without your spouse with you, and no friendships with anyone you are attracted to unless it is the spouse of another friend and you are never alone with him or her. There can be no exceptions to this rule.

WE ARE NOT ANIMALS

We are people, not animals, so we can control our basest instincts. Sure, you're going to have feelings for other people, even fantasize about them from time to time. I've had mind sex with just about every starlet in Hollywood and more than one total babe that I've met in the course of my daily routine. But when I feel tempted, I just close my eyes and imagine how my daughter's hair smells when she snuggles in my lap, or how my wife and I laugh until it hurts every day, and most of all, how they have all stuck by me, a pretty difficult guy, since the beginning. Then I try to imagine life every day without them, and believe me, the sex fantasy disappears like magic! Just keep it a fantasy. Your life will be simpler, your family happier, your lawyer poorer, and you will be the happiest one of all!

HERBISM: THE REASON SOCIETY HAS RULES IS BECAUSE THEY WORK. THEY PROTECT US ALL AND AT THE SAME TIME LEAD TO LONG-LASTING HAPPINESS.

40
WHAT IT ALL MEANS

(...AND HOW YOU'LL KNOW THE DIFFERENCE)

Whew! You and I have finally reached the end of this, our first journey together. I hope it's been as much fun for you as it has for me.

When I set out to write this book, I decided to write a different kind of business book, one that addresses lifestyle choices as well as the money issues. Heck, I've read so many books that were like watching paint dry that I refused to write one of my own just to call myself an author. No, if I was going to do this, as Frank Sinatra said, I was going to do it My Way.

So I've tried to deliver my message to you in the most complete and adult way possible, by talking about success and failure and all the things we do as humans to make a real mess of it. And I've tried to do it in plain English, not some academic mush. I hope you've enjoyed the result.

180   Harold Kushner wrote in his terrific book *When Bad Things Happen to Good People* that without sadness there can be no happiness. Otherwise, how would you ever know the difference? Making it big in life is no different. Success is not possible without the possibility of failure. The danger is what makes the fruit so sweet.

Let me close with an admission. Everything that you will ever need to know about business and success is not in this book, or even in a thousand more just like it. Your experiences will be uniquely your own, and the only way to get past the problems and roll up the victories is to get going.

As Frederick the Great said: "De l'audace, encore de l'audace, et toujours de l'audace!" ("Boldness, again boldness, always boldness!")

So — what are you waiting for?

HERBISM: NO GUTS, NO GLORY. THE TIME FOR ACTION IS NOW!

INDEX

ABOUT HERB KAY, LLC

(THINGS YOU SHOULD KNOW ABOUT HERB'S COMPANY)

Herb Kay is the managing partner and founder of Herb Kay, LLC. The National Association of Securities Dealers currently licenses him as a registered representative and principal. Affiliated with Linsco/Private Ledger (LPL), one of the largest independent brokerage firms in the United States and member of the Securities Investor Protection Corporation, Herb currently manages the private investment accounts of individuals and companies throughout the United States. In conjunction with his investment practice, Herb has received numerous awards, including LPL's prestigious Chairman's and Patriot's Club honors for outstanding customer service and high production. Herb has hosted a syndicated TV financial talk show, appears regularly as a financial expert on various national television programs, is in demand as a speaker for corporate and civic groups, and writes a weekly newspaper column. On top of all of this, he is currently developing condominiums in Mexico and building a restaurant in Puerto Peñasco, Sonora. He has several other projects under development.